The Peace Corps Today

The Peace Corps Today

Merni Ingrassia Fitzgerald

Illustrated with photographs

Dodd, Mead & Company
New York

This book is dedicated to Toni and Jaimi

PICTURE CREDITS

Ann Arbor News (Eckstanger), 14; Jeff Hankins, 48; Deborah Hollis, 49; George Whitney, 115. All other photographs are Peace Corps photographs.

The "starfish" story on page 23 is used with permission of the Minnesota Literacy Council, Inc., and reprinted with permission from the September, 1984, *Reader's Digest*.

Copyright © 1986 by Merni Ingrassia Fitzgerald
All rights reserved
No part of this book may be reproduced in any form without permission in writing from the publisher
Distributed in Canada by
McClelland and Stewart Limited, Toronto
Manufactured in the United States of America
Designed by Annie Alleman
1 2 3 4 5 6 7 8 9 10
Library of Congress Cataloging-in-Publication Data
Fitzgerald, Merni Ingrassia.
  The Peace Corps today.
    Includes index.
    Summary: Describes the history and purpose of the Peace Corps, its work today, and how one can become a volunteer. Includes quotations from volunteers recounting their experiences in various countries.
    1. Peace Corps (U.S.)—Juvenile literature.
  [1. Peace Corps (U.S.)]   I. Title.
  HC60.5.F585   1986   361.2'6'06073   85-29396
  ISBN 0-396-08511-3

ACKNOWLEDGMENTS

The author wishes to acknowledge the gracious cooperation and assistance of current and former members of the Peace Corps staff. Stan Schrager, Hugh O'Neill, Anne Alvarez, Casey Bean, Martha Saldinger, and Chuck Wattles are but a few of the many people who made her job easier.

The author also wishes to acknowledge Loret Miller Ruppe, Peace Corps Director, who saw the need for a children's book about today's Peace Corps.

Special thanks to all the returned Peace Corps volunteers who responded to the author's questionnaire, or discussed their Peace Corps volunteer experiences with her.

Foreword

My congratulations to the author, Merni Fitzgerald, for her excellent telling of the Peace Corps story and to you, the reader, for choosing a subject so important to today's world.

The Peace Corps began as the dream of Americans concerned about world peace and the need to help others. My hope is that as you read about how our program became a reality, you will also dare to dream—about a world without hunger and war. In twenty-five years Peace Corps volunteers have seen the introduction of satellite television that brought the world closer together. This shows us that we live in a "global village," where television cameras bring us together within a matter of minutes. However, to truly bring the world together, we, as Americans, must learn the languages of others, understand their cultures, and share our skills.

I am pleased to say that today more and more Americans are in the Peace Corps. Young and old have joined together to accept our challenge to make the world a better place.

Be proud of the accomplishments of America's Peace Corps volunteers. I hope you will consider Peace Corps service at some time in your life. It is truly the "toughest job you'll ever love."

Loret Miller Ruppe
Peace Corps Director

Contents

Foreword by Loret Miller Ruppe *vi*

1. The Birth of the Peace Corps *11*
2. The Peace Corps Today *24*
3. Helping Women Around the World *38*
4. Information Collection and Exchange (ICE) *46*
5. How to Become a Peace Corps Volunteer *50*
6. "Dear Mom and Dad and Timmy" *63*
7. Returned Peace Corps Volunteers *83*
8. It's a Small World *91*
9. Peace Corps Partnership Program *103*
10. How *You* Can Help the Peace Corps *113*

Index *126*

The United States of America

is pleased to announce the birth of

Name:

Date: March 1, 1961

Parents: President John F. Kennedy
U. S. Congress

Grandparents: William James
International Voluntary Services
Dr. James H. Robinson
Members of Congress: Congressman Henry Reuss and Senator Hubert H. Humphrey

Vital Statistics: Defined by Congress on September 22, 1961, when the Peace Corps Act was passed, outlining the three goals

First Steps Taken: September 12, 1961, when Tom Livingston of Woodale, Illinois, became the first Peace Corps volunteer on duty

-1-
The Birth of the Peace Corps

What is the Peace Corps? Why does it send Americans to faraway countries, to live and work in villages or towns with people speaking another language? Why have over 100,000 Americans served as volunteers since the Peace Corps was born in 1961?

To answer these questions, we have to look back at the history of our country. Since the first settlers landed on the shores of America, people have helped their neighbors and friends. Not merely by donating extra tools, food, or goods, but by giving of themselves—working alongside others building schools, clearing the land for a log cabin, or teaching children to read. No money or payment was received or expected; the reward was the satisfaction of working side-by-side with other people, helping to improve their lives.

Acting upon the words of the American philosopher William James, who suggested that America should join an army to fight against disease and poverty, a large group of young American volunteers taught English in the Philippines in 1901. They sailed on the USS *Thomas*, and were known as the Thomasites.

After World War II, many new countries were formed throughout the world. The people in these countries were not rich, and needed help building schools and bridges, bringing water to deserts, planting trees, and teaching their children. America's spirit of helping others prompted different groups to extend a helping hand to these neighbors around the globe. Often, the help was in the form of food, supplies, and medicine.

More needed to be done, so religious organizations and private agencies sent volunteers to work with the people overseas in self-improvement projects. In 1953, International Voluntary Services was formed in the United States as a private, nonprofit organization. It sent volunteers from the U.S. and other countries overseas to work in public health and farming projects, house building and home economics.

Dr. James H. Robinson, a black minister and Director of Morningside Community Center in New York City, and sixty students spent the summer of 1958 in Africa working on community projects for "Operation Crossroads," a private group which he founded. By 1963, this agency had 304 students

The Birth of the Peace Corps 13

Peace Corps volunteer with a friend in Sierra Leone

working on 27 projects in 19 countries. Both International Voluntary Services and "Operation Crossroads" exist today, sending volunteers to other countries to provide assistance to people who are less fortunate than themselves.

Those earlier efforts paved the way for the birth of the Peace Corps. Some people, including Congressional leaders, foresaw a federal government agency that sent volunteers to help needy people overseas. On January 14, 1960, Congressman Henry Reuss (Democrat, Wisconsin) introduced a bill in the House of Representatives for a study of a "Point Four Youth Corps" plan. It was passed. As early as 1957, Senator Hubert H. Humphrey (Democrat, Minnesota) started talking to college graduates about a "youth peace corps" and raised the idea of an international voluntary program in the primary elections of 1960. John F. Kennedy was the winner in those elections, but Humphrey introduced a "peace corps" bill in the Senate in June, 1960. So he was the first person to use the name "Peace Corps." Although Humphrey's bill did not pass, Kennedy used many of his ideas later when the Peace Corps was actually formed.

President John F. Kennedy is credited as the founder of the Peace Corps. On October 14, 1960, after an exhausting day spent campaigning for the presidency, Kennedy spoke to University of Michigan students on the steps of the University Student Union in Ann Arbor, Michigan.

"How many of you are willing to spend ten years in Africa or Latin America or Asia working for the United States and working for freedom? How many of you who are going to be doctors are willing to spend your days in Ghana; technicians or engineers,

John F. Kennedy proposed the Peace Corps during a campaign speech at the University of Michigan.

The Birth of the Peace Corps 15

how many of you are willing to work in the foreign service and spend your lives traveling around the world?"

In Ghana a volunteer attempts to balance a pail of millet on her head as the village women do.

Sargent Shriver served as Director of the Peace Corps from 1961 to 1966.

He concluded by saying, "I think Americans *are* willing to contribute, but the effort must be far greater than we have made in the past."

The idea for the Peace Corps caught the imagination of the American people, young and old, and when Kennedy became President, he began the process leading to the birth of the Peace Corps. As in any birth, preparations must be made for the new arrival. President Kennedy appointed his brother-in-law, Sargent Shriver, as head of a group to study the formation of a Peace Corps.

Although there were many missionary and private organizations' experiences to examine and learn from, the Peace Corps was a new idea. So as the preparations continued, many questions arose. Who would take care of the health of the volunteers when they were working overseas? Would married couples be accepted as volunteers? Where would the training take place, in America or overseas? How would the volunteers be chosen from the many qualified people who wanted to join the Peace Corps? Despite the public support for the idea, would anyone actually be willing to serve in a country 10,000 miles away, halfway around the world?

Names are often debated and discussed before a birth, and the name of the Peace Corps was no exception. Some people thought the use of the word "peace" was too corny. Others believed that "corps" brought to mind the military. But the name was kept. After all, the corps of volunteers

The Birth of the Peace Corps 17

President John F. Kennedy signs the Executive Order creating the Peace Corps.

across the globe would bring peace by working to eliminate the conditions that bring about war— poverty, disease, sickness, and disaster.

After many hours of work, consulting with experts and reviewing the many suggestions received, Sargent Shriver recommended that the Peace Corps be established immediately.

The Peace Corps was officially born on March 1, 1961, when President Kennedy signed the Executive Order. Tom Livingston of Woodale, Illinois, is credited as being the first Peace Corps volunteer on duty, since he was the first to step off the plane in Ghana on September 12, 1961, from among the 51 teachers who flew there to serve in secondary school education programs. Mr. Livingston became an English teacher at Ghanata Secondary School in the small village of Dowdowa, Ghana, in West Africa.

The purposes of the Peace Corps were defined in the Peace Corps Act which was passed by the United States Congress on September 22, 1961. The three goals are:

- To help the people of interested countries and areas in meeting their needs for trained manpower
- To help promote a better understanding of Americans on the part of the peoples served
- To help promote a better understanding of other peoples on the part of the American people

From the beginning the appeal of the Peace Corps for young people has not only been the opportunity for service, but the chance to get to know another country. Tourists also travel to far-off countries, visiting famous landmarks and possibly learning local history and sampling foods, but very few tourists leave the American-style hotels to live among the local people. Few tourists have the time or interest to learn to speak the local language, respect the culture, and discover the local customs, art, and literature.

The Birth of the Peace Corps 19

Peace Corps volunteers get this chance. As guests of the welcoming country, they discover that dress and behavior which is perfectly acceptable in the United States is not necessarily correct elsewhere. In living in a new country, Peace Corps volunteers must be sensitive to the tastes and habits of the people.

Peace Corps volunteers represent not only the Peace Corps, but also the United States. President John F. Kennedy saw Peace Corps volunteers as "ambassadors of peace." Peace Corps volunteers are sometimes the only view of America for people in their host countries.

"Host country" means the country in which the Peace Corps volunteer serves. The Peace Corps

Tom Livingston was in this first group of volunteers that went to Ghana in 1961.

does not send any volunteers into a country unless their services have been requested. Peace Corps volunteers are invited guests in other countries. It's like guests coming to dinner at your house. Your parents are the hosts, offering their home and food to the invited guests. The people in host countries are offering their homes, food, and friendship to Peace Corps volunteers.

> "I had a very difficult time making friends at first. I was lonely for someone who could speak my own language. Before I left I'd always thought it was rude for foreigners to speak their native tongue in front of English-speaking people . . . I thought they were keeping secrets from us. But now whenever I saw anyone who could speak English, it was 'Please talk English with me!' "
>
> Peace Corps volunteer
> Togo

The Peace Corps experience has had real effects on both the volunteers and the countries they served. Sometimes it is hard to measure the contribution of a Peace Corps volunteer. Volunteers do not bring heavy machinery, or expensive equipment. They bring their hands, hearts, knowledge, and dedication.

The Birth of the Peace Corps 21

Supervising construction of a well in Togo

The meaning of the Peace Corps can be found in this old Chinese proverb: "If you give a man a fish, he will have a meal. If you teach a man to fish, he will eat all his life." Instead of just bringing things to give to the people of the host country, volunteers teach the people how to better themselves, so that when the volunteer leaves to return home to the United States, the people will be able to continue living a better life.

The experience of entering a new country as a Peace Corps volunteer is like that of a foreign student when entering an American school. Communication is difficult at first until the new language is learned.

It is sometimes difficult in the beginning to leave friends and family behind. Sounds, smells, and sights are new and exciting. You look and sound dif-

---

"I'll never forget the look on the children's faces when I was walking through town being introduced. Every one of the small children took one look at me and it was almost as if they'd seen a ghost or something like that. Their eyes grew so wide and they ran as fast as they could around the corner."

Peace Corps volunteer
Sierra Leone

ferent from everyone else, and that can be a strange feeling.

But with time, Peace Corps volunteers come to a deeper understanding. As a returned Peace Corps volunteer noted: "It's said so many times and you hear it in words and songs, but people really are basically the same all around the world . . ."

A great dream was realized when the Peace Corps was born in 1961. When we try to measure the total impact of this birth around the world, for millions of people faraway, an old Chinese proverb again comes to mind: "A journey of a thousand miles begins with a single step."

Or, to put it another way, there is this story by an anonymous author:

As the old man walked the beach at dawn, he noticed a young man ahead of him picking up starfish and flinging them into the sea. Finally catching up with the youth, he asked him why he was doing this. The answer was that the stranded starfish would die if left until the morning sun.

"But the beach goes on for miles and there are millions of starfish," countered the other. "How can your effort make any difference?"

The young man looked at the starfish in his hand and then threw it to safety in the waves.

"It makes a difference to this one," he said.

-2-
The Peace Corps Today

The Peace Corps is alive and healthy in the 1980s. Despite growing pains, it has survived and grown. In 1961, when the Peace Corps was founded, volunteers served in nine countries. Since that time over 100,000 volunteers have served in 91 different countries. Today, in a single month, more than one million lives are directly touched by Peace Corps volunteers at work in as many as 60 countries around the world.

But Peace Corps volunteers today are different from volunteers of twenty years ago. In the early days, most volunteers were young college students. Today, they range in age from eighteen to over seventy. Back then, grade school education was not available to most children in developing countries. Peace Corps volunteers serving as teachers have given thousands of these children a chance to go to school. Today, most children in foreign countries

This volunteer introduced beekeeping to the people of Montserrat in the Caribbean.

attend schools, many of which were built with the help of a Peace Corps volunteer. So schoolteachers are not needed as much as they once were.

Peace Corps volunteers today still work with the people in their host country, but they are working in different projects than before. Many volunteers still teach, but some of them are teaching skills for improving people's lives outside a classroom setting, such as improved cooking techniques. Peace Corps volunteers do the following, and more:

- Build ponds so that people can have fish to eat
- Teach people to build mud stoves
- Work on crocodile farms
- Plant trees
- Help sell the handicrafts made by villagers
- Organize Special Olympics games, where disabled persons compete in sports events
- Teach sign language to deaf children and adults
- Teach people the science of beekeeping

All kinds of Americans serve as Peace Corps volunteers. Married couples can both become volunteers. Many retired men and women use their knowledge and skills to serve in the Peace Corps. An 81-year-old volunteer works in Haiti, a country in the Caribbean, helping build schools for the people of that country. There is no upper age limit for joining the Peace Corps, so you can't be too old to apply. Many host countries greatly respect and honor older persons. Minorities are welcome. The Peace Corps is for all Americans: Asian, Black, Hispanic, Native, and White—male and female, old and young. Most minority groups in the United States have roots in Africa, Asia, and many Spanish-

Opposite page: There is no age limit for Peace Corps volunteers. At over eighty, this volunteer served in Sierra Leone.

The Peace Corps Today 27

28   THE PEACE CORPS TODAY

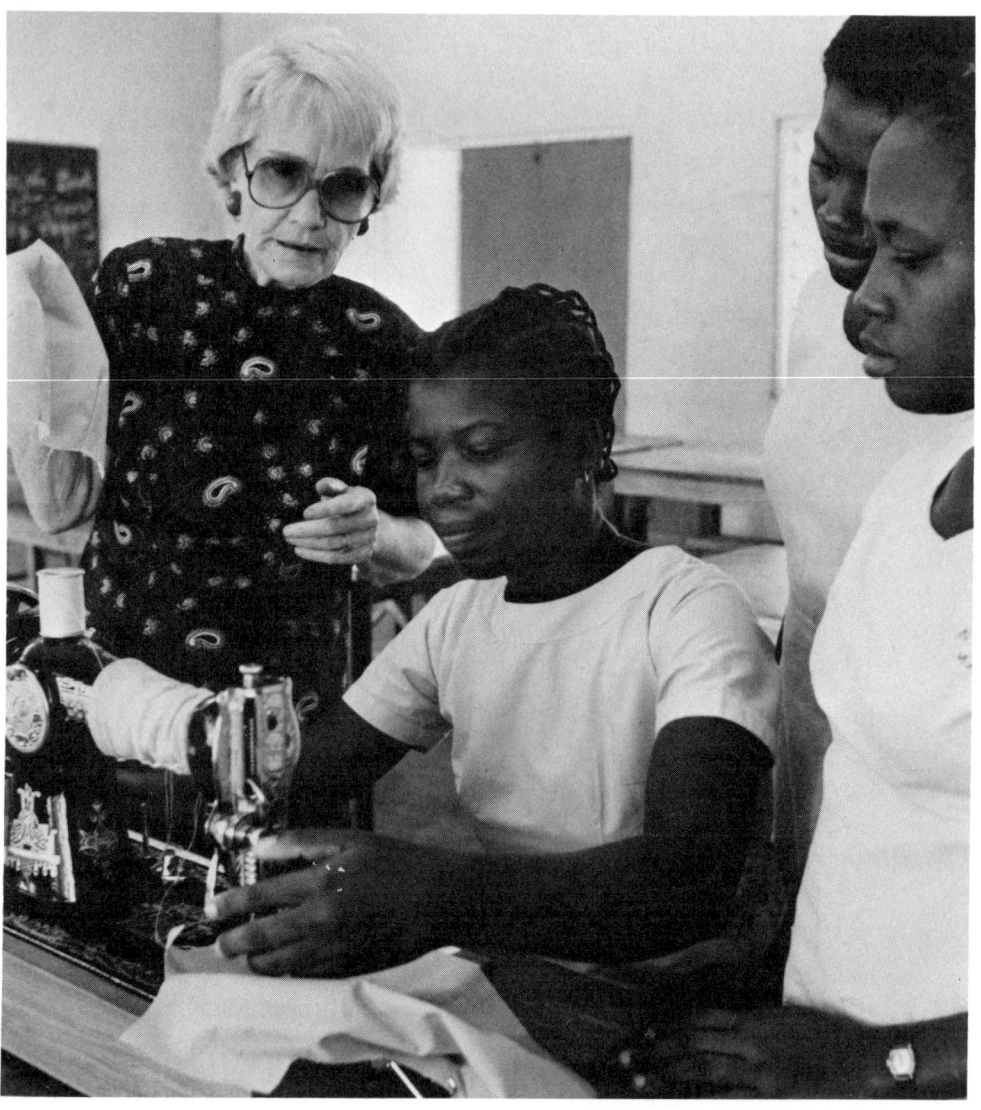

This volunteer teaches dressmaking, as well as math and English, in Ghana.

The Peace Corps Today 29

In Thailand, volunteers examine a carp from a fisheries demonstration pond.

30 THE PEACE CORPS TODAY

A volunteer in Niger gets her hair dressed by a neighbor.

speaking countries. Host countries often ask, "Where are your people who look like us?"

The world has changed a lot since 1961. Many new countries have been born, and there are over 1 billion more people now than there were then. The Peace Corps has changed too, but it remains an important program today, helping people overseas meet their needs for food, shelter, and health care.

Peace Corps volunteers join today for the same reasons as before—a desire to help people, to learn about new countries, to travel to far-off places, and to share skills and knowledge.

"I'd like to think I am going to change the world and make life better for everyone," said one Peace Corps volunteer. "I know I'm not going to accomplish that much. My main goal will be to help more people become qualified in math and physics and to learn about a different culture."

The Peace Corps is not in all the same countries it was in back in 1961. The number of countries and the places vary from year to year. The Peace Corps has left countries it once served, and entered new countries. There are several reasons for leaving a country. Sometimes the need for which the volunteers were asked to serve in the first place no longer exists. The Peace Corps left Malaysia in 1983 because the volunteers had "worked themselves out of a job." Malaysians were able to take over the jobs done by the volunteers, so the successful Peace Corps program was ended.

The Peace Corps has had a large effect on America, as well as on many other countries across the globe. The children of Peace Corps volunteers who served in the early 1960s are now adults, and some are entering the Peace Corps themselves. Over 100,000 Americans have served in the Peace Corps

The Peace Corps Around the World

date: May, 1985

34 THE PEACE CORPS TODAY

and returned to this country with a new awareness of life in another country, a new knowledge of a foreign language, a new self-sufficiency obtained from their two years of service. Many are holding positions of responsibility, serving as college presidents, Senators, Congressmen, and presidents of large companies.

This effect can be likened to swimming or playing in a lake, when a motorboat passes by through the deep water beyond you. The boat is not at all close

A volunteer from North Carolina serves as a physical education specialist in Barbados.

to you, but eventually the ripples and small waves it causes reach you. The Peace Corps volunteer is like the motorboat, touching people in their host country and here in America in areas far from where they actually live. As the motorboat sends ripples to the outer ends of the lake, so do Peace Corps volunteers send ripples across the world.

This ripple effect can be seen when an African country leader draws upon the knowledge he received as a schoolboy from a Peace Corps volunteer.

> "I had been in Malaysia for quite some time when I got the chance to use a washing machine to clean my dirty laundry. Having forgotten how to use modern-day machines such as a washer, I put in too much laundry detergent. The machine exploded with suds!"
>
> **Peace Corps volunteer**
> **Malaysia**

The people in that country benefit now from the work of a Peace Corps teacher twenty years earlier. Or in this country, enthusiasm and interest are kindled in many people who view an exhibit of Ecuadorian artifacts set up in the local library by a returned Peace Corps volunteer who served in Ecuador.

A student newspaper in Nigeria, Africa, wrote about the Peace Corps volunteers who were getting ready to leave and return home to America. "Now that these men and women have almost completed their tour and are preparing to leave, we feel that no amount of praise showered on them for their work is too much. To our Peace Corps friends about to leave us, we say, we are indeed sorry to see you go. We shall miss you and your services. In the meantime, we say *Se Wa Tarana*, which is the Hausa meaning for 'Good-bye: We shall see you again.'"

On February 1, 1983, the Peace Corps volunteers and staff in the Philippine Islands were awarded the Golden Heart Presidential Award, the highest award ever given to anyone not from the Philippines. It honored the Peace Corps as an important part of the long friendship and understanding between the Philippines and the United States of America.

Loret Miller Ruppe, appointed Peace Corps Director in 1981, has said: "The Peace Corps is an American program that people [overseas] are grateful for. Here is a program that is a proven success story. When I went to Jamaica, the Prime Minister insisted on getting up from his sick bed to see me and thank me for the Peace Corps. Even the newspapers there had articles thanking America for the Peace Corps."

According to a chief of a tribe in Sierra Leone, the Peace Corps showed his people ". . . a world we never knew existed. We had never seen people from the outside who wanted to help us. We had heard of America, but now we know what it means." The Peace Corps in the eighties is still fulfilling the dreams of yesterday, while keeping up with the people and needs of today.

In the Philippines a volunteer teaches hand language to deaf nursery school children.

-3-
Helping Women Around the World

How can the seedlings planted as part of a Peace Corps forestry project in the African country of Sierra Leone live and grow into strong trees?

By getting the *women* of Sierra Leone involved in the project.

How can the fish caught in Guatemala, a country in Central America, reach the market and earn extra money for the fishermen and their families?

By getting the *women* of Guatemala involved in the project.

The women in these countries are the key to the success of the two projects. In seeking to better the lives of people overseas, today's Peace Corps volunteers are paying more attention to the women.

When only men worked on the Sierra Leone forestry project, the seedlings died from lack of water and care. The men said that carrying water was women's work. The women knew the importance of having wood close to their village, and so they wanted the project to be a success. When the Peace Corps volunteer included the women as workers to tend the plants, the seedlings lived and grew.

Talking with women in Sierra Leone

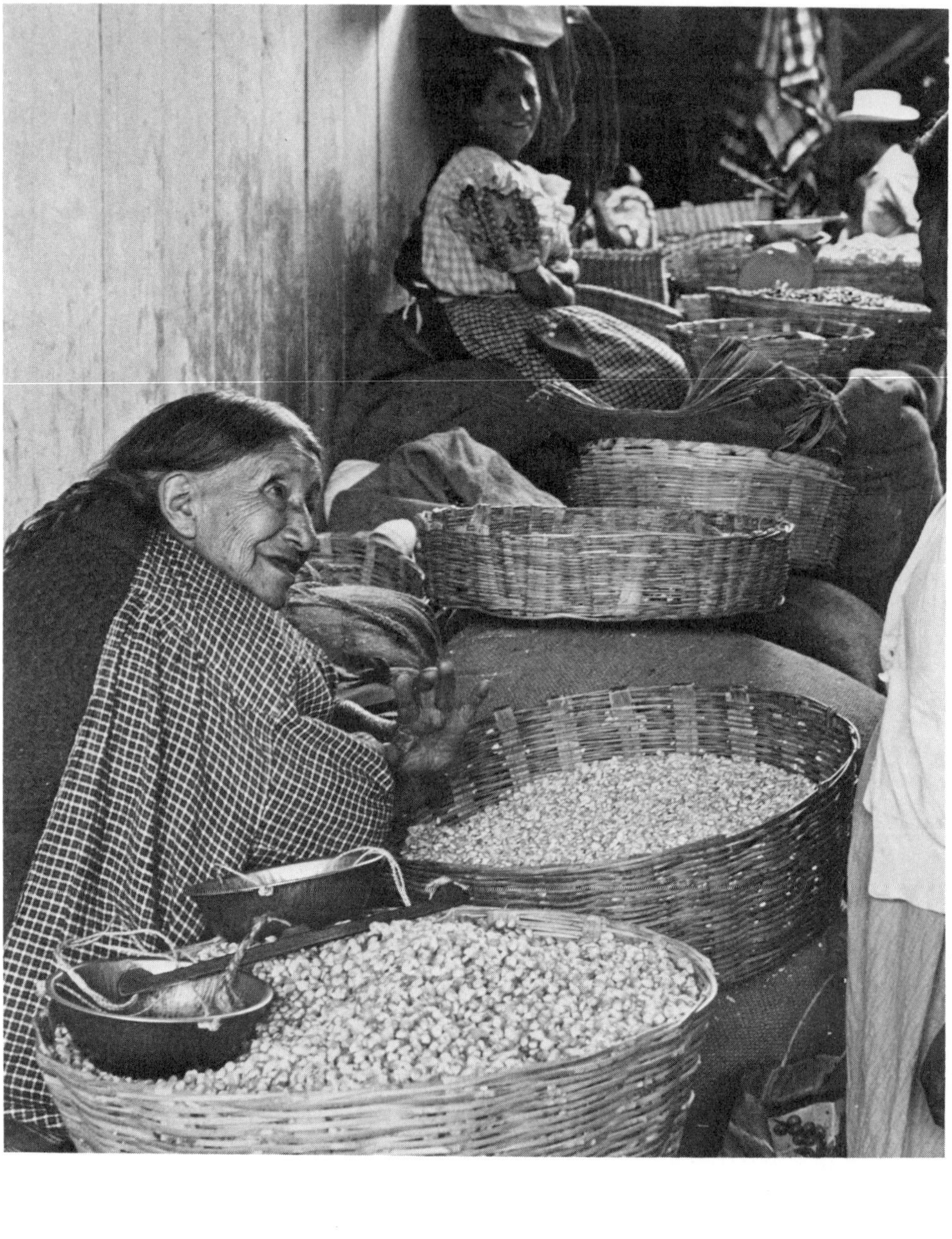

The impact of women was the same in Guatemala with the fisheries project. When the Peace Corps volunteer made sure that women, who usually cleaned, preserved, and sold the fish, became involved, the project became a success.

Opposite page: Guatemalan women selling their wares in the marketplace

> "It was late afternoon in Togo, West Africa. I was tired from a long day spent teaching at the local school, and knew I had to gather wood and draw water before I could prepare my dinner of rice, tomato sauce, and dried fish bones. But I waited for a young friend of mine, who had promised to share something with me for my meal. I laughed to myself as I sat waiting, remembering my mistake of the day before. Some tiny green leaves had caught my attention at the market. I bought them, with visions of a delicious salad for my evening meal. As I washed the greens, I ignored the red water that dripped from the leaves. The market wouldn't sell food unless it was able to be eaten, right? This morning I discovered that the leaves were only used to dye toenails and fingernails red! My young friend arrived then, holding out her hand to give me her gift. Roasted June bugs! Hamburgers and French fries had never seemed so far away."
>
> Peace Corps volunteer
> Togo

The Peace Corps calls this focus on the women in the host countries "Women in Development."

Opposite page: Women in Cameroon are assisted in organizing women's groups to learn about hygiene, mother-child care, cooking, nutrition.

"Women in Development" is not a program, it is not a support group for female volunteers, and it is not for or by women only. It is a focus on women's roles and needs, and an acknowledgment that women are full members of every community.

Senator Charles Percy supported legislation recognizing "Women in Development" for many years in Congress. An amendment, attached to the Foreign Assistance Act, was finally passed. Known as the Percy Amendment, it directed all federal government agencies to recognize the important role women played in the development process. Accordingly, an amendment was added to the Peace Corps Act in 1978:

"In recognition of the fact that women in developing countries play a significant role in economic production, family support, and the overall development process, the Peace Corps shall be administered so as to give particular attention to those programs, projects, and activities which tend to integrate women into the national economies of developing countries, thus improving their status and assisting the total development effort."

How has the Peace Corps helped women in the countries it serves? In Ecuador, a country in South America, women have obtained small grants to set up village businesses, with the assistance of Peace Corps volunteers. These businesses include village stores, a local bakery, and poultry projects. When the bakery threatened to close because the women did not feel comfortable selling their baked goods, which is traditionally a man's job, the women turned their efforts to egg production.

> "I was to deliver 800 laying hens to village poultry units on another island. While waiting for the ferry and then again as we were crossing the channel, chickens constantly wiggled their way to freedom despite our numerous efforts to block all escape routes. So for four hours my driver and I scurried about the dock and ferry chasing chickens while bystanders either had a great time watching our plight and pointing out the latest 'escapee' or joined in on the 'great chicken chase' with us. In the end, the only losses were those that had died from exhaustion in their useless efforts to escape our clutches."
>
> Peace Corps volunteer
Western Samoa

In Nepal, a country between China and India, the Peace Corps volunteers work with the Nepalese people to help farm women get credit from local banks for raising animals. The women are using their skills working with goats and buffalo to earn money.

Peace Corps volunteers in Morocco, a country in northern Africa, help train women as welders, teaching them skills that will help them obtain much-needed jobs.

In Sierra Leone, Guatemala, Ecuador, Nepal, and Morocco the Peace Corps has been able to help the communities because they helped the women. This special focus is part of all Peace Corps projects around the world.

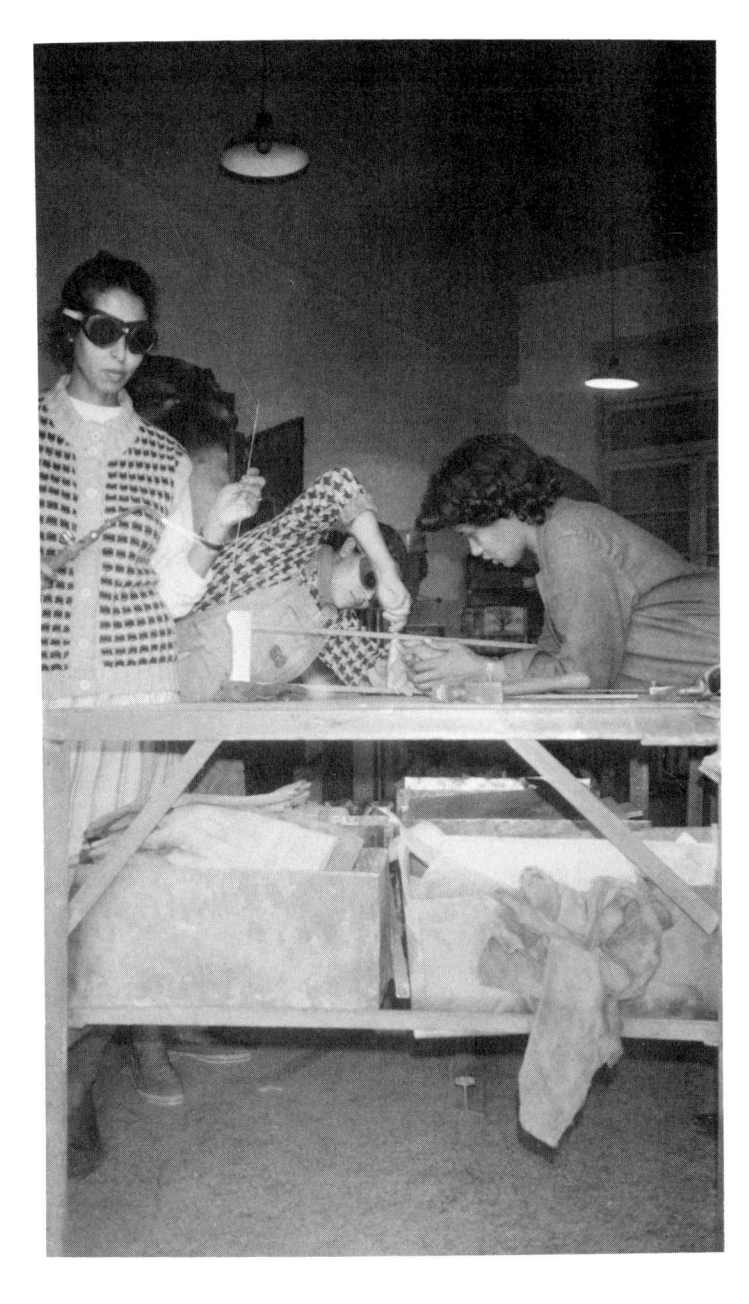

Women in Morocco assemble crutches.

-4-
Information Collection and Exchange (ICE)

A Peace Corps volunteer in Tonga, an island nation in the South Pacific, developed new projects for his students in an industrial arts class. One project was the construction of a kerosene lantern. Tongans who did not have electricity or could not afford their own commercial lanterns needed kerosene lanterns. Their homemade lanterns produced a dull flame and much smoke. The volunteer taught his students how to make a lantern out of a used tuna can, an old bottle, some sheet metal and a cotton wick, and a piece of rubber from a "flip-flop" sandal. It worked very well, and did not cost much to make.

Fourteen months later, in the Philippine Islands, another Peace Corps volunteer wanted to make a cheap kerosene lantern. You might say, "It's too bad the Peace Corps volunteer in Tonga can't share his lantern design and instructions with the Peace Corps volunteer in the Philippines."

Opposite page: A volunteer in the Philippines at his bamboo house.

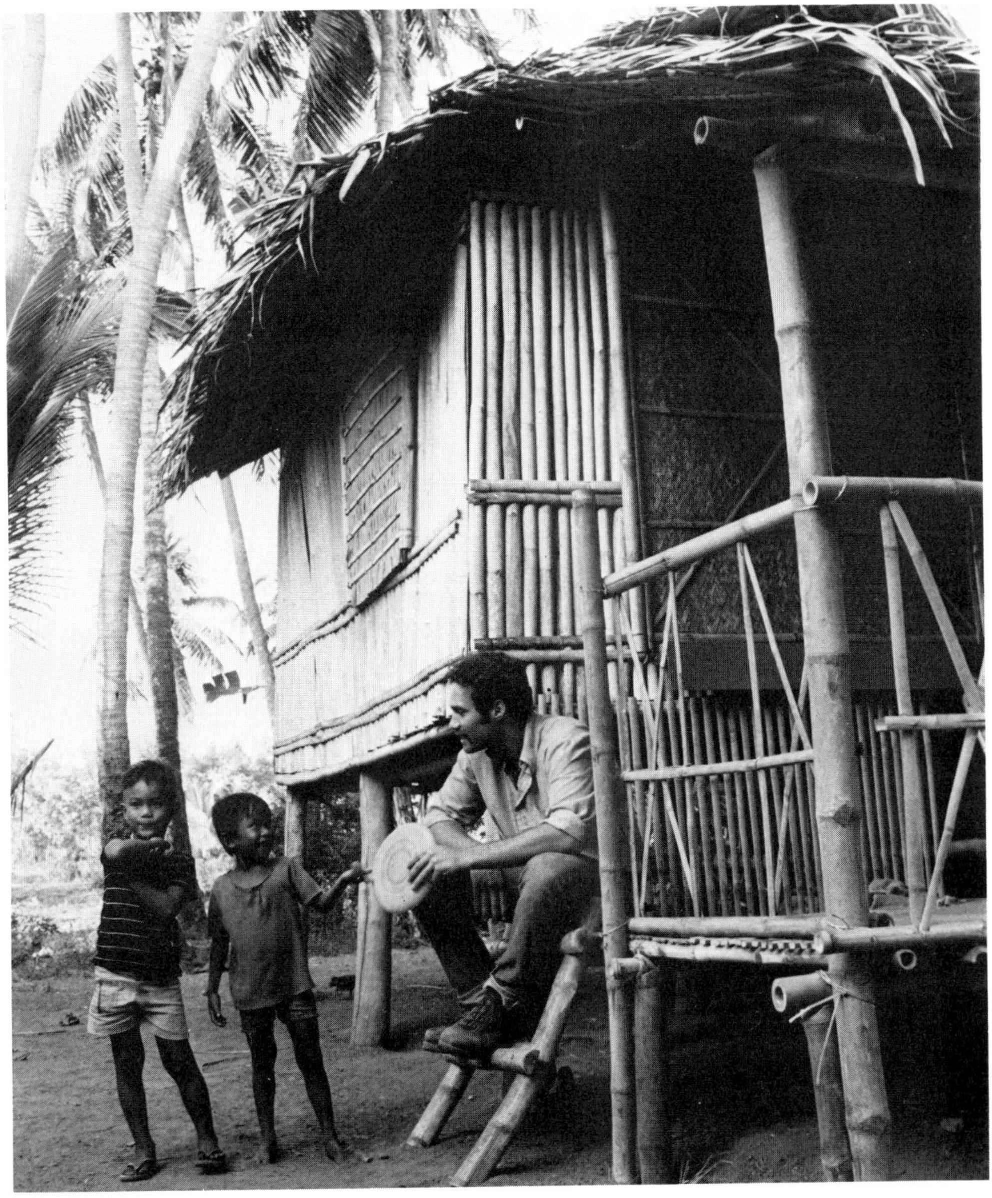

48   THE PEACE CORPS TODAY

Thanks to the Information Collection and Exchange (ICE) program in today's Peace Corps, this is possible. This program collects information from volunteers and distributes it to other volunteers around the world. The information is in the form of manuals, or it appears in the ICE Almanac section of the publication for volunteers, the *Peace Corps Times*. This magazine is published by the Peace Corps staff in Washington, D.C., six times a year. It is distributed to volunteers in their host countries, to all United States Representatives and Senators, to other international development organizations, and to former volunteers who specifically request it.

The main purpose of the *Peace Corps Times* is to serve the volunteers, bringing them news about the Peace Corps in featured countries, activities of the director and staff, and other helpful information. The *Peace Corps Times* always contains the ICE Almanac, which features a variety of volunteer ideas and listings of various publications that are available to volunteers and staff through the ICE office. Thus, new programs, detailed instructions, and special teaching techniques need not be lost when a Peace Corps volunteer returns home.

The volunteer in the Philippines was able to make the inexpensive kerosene lantern after receiving instructions from ICE. Volunteers in 60 countries around the world are able to make the same lantern, thanks to ICE. One Peace Corps volunteer's knowledge and experience help people in many, many places.

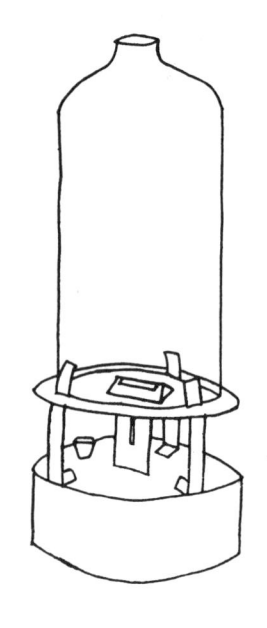

Drawing of kerosene lantern made by volunteer in Tonga appeared in ICE Almanac with instructions for making it.

ICE also helps volunteers communicate with Peace Corps volunteers in other countries. Several years ago, ICE set up the Volunteer-to-Volunteer Network. From time to time, the ICE Almanac in the *Peace Corps Times* publishes a questionnaire for volunteers to complete and return. Then, ICE sends the list of potential "pen pals" to the volunteers or publishes the list in the Almanac. So a Peace Corps volunteer working as a dental hygienist in one country can correspond with a volunteer dental hygienist in another country.

A volunteer in Mali helped women build simple stoves of sand and mud—and let other volunteers know how in ICE Almanac.

Volunteers, although busy with their projects, often have time at night to write to their families, to other volunteers, or to jot off a note to ICE about a new way to make or do something that will benefit other volunteers around the world.

"Well, it finally happened. I've had dogs, cats, chickens, goats, birds, and a wide variety of insects find their way into my classes (I have no doors or windows and a dirt floor). But a full-grown bull? I didn't know what to do, so I just stopped talking and stared back. The kids picked up stones and chunks of cow dung off the floor and pulled stones out of the walls which they threw at the bull. It worked, because the bull just grunted and wandered back out of the classroom. Now that I think back on it, that was one, hilarious experience."

Peace Corps volunteer
Kenya

-5-
How to Become a Peace Corps Volunteer

So you want to be a Peace Corps volunteer? You would be willing to give up your new bike and computer, learn another language, eat new foods, live in a mud hut, and miss your favorite television shows? You want to travel to faraway places, and become an accepted member of the village or community there? You want to follow in the footsteps of over 100,000 fellow Americans who have served in other countries helping people help themselves?

The good news is that you join thousands of other Americans who at this very minute share your wish to be a Peace Corps volunteer. The bad news is that you have to be eighteen years old before you can apply to be in the Peace Corps.

However, there aren't too many other rules. You must be a United States citizen. You must be healthy. You must be willing to serve for two years. You will receive training in the local language, as well as in the beliefs and values of other countries. Although you don't get paid for your time as a volunteer, you will receive money for your housing, food, travel, and any medicine that is needed. A readjustment allowance will be set aside each month for you, payable when you complete your Peace Corps service.

Not everyone who wants to be a Peace Corps volunteer actually becomes one. About one out of every seven people who apply to the Peace Corps are ac-

---

"Soon after I became a Peace Corps volunteer, I went to a beautiful village in the mountains of Honduras to visit a friend. My Spanish was still poor; there were many words I had not yet learned. One evening I went to my room to get ready for bed, only to find a little chick standing on my pillow. City slicker that I am, I was terrified of trying to pick the chick up. I ran out of my room, trying to say 'There's a chicken in my room.' I wanted one of the neighbor children who were visiting my friend to get rid of the chick. In my panic I yelled *'Hay un ave en mi cuarto.'* The word *'ave'* is only used to refer to very large birds! My friend and the kids were stunned and sneaked up to my doorway to see what monstrous bird had taken over the room. When they saw the chick they burst out laughing! They called me Ana de Pollito (Ann of the Chick) for the rest of my stay!"

Peace Corps volunteer
Honduras

cepted. Let's meet one person who made it through the whole process. Let's call her Maria Sanchez.

Maria was born twenty-nine years ago in California, and moved to Wauwatosa, Wisconsin, with her family when she was five. She has lived there since then, and now shares her apartment with a yellow, tabby cat. Maria works as an editor for the newsletter at the New Energy Woodstove Company. One night she stayed up past midnight to watch the late movie. Maria was getting very tired as the time neared 2:00 A.M. and had almost fallen asleep when the music of a commercial startled her. Maria sat up in her chair and listened as she watched someone on horseback discussing "the toughest job you'll ever love."

It finally dawned on her sleepy mind that the ad was for the Peace Corps.

"Is that still around?" Maria asked herself as she nestled deeper into her cozy rocking chair, and promptly fell asleep.

Maria dreamed that she was a Peace Corps volunteer riding a horse as she herded cattle into the gates of a ranch. Maria was cranky when she woke up the next morning, due to lack of sleep. As she drank her third cup of coffee she muttered to herself: "What a crazy dream! I can't even ride a horse!"

The Peace Corps ad soon haunted her daytime hours, however, and Maria decided to get more information about becoming a Peace Corps volunteer.

Opposite page: This volunteer in Sierra Leone takes time out to play with her pet chimpanzee.

How to Become a Peace Corps Volunteer 53

> "In East Africa, four friends and I rented a car to take us from place to place, seeing the sights. We couldn't find anyplace to spend the night, so we slept in the car with the window down partway. I was peacefully asleep when suddenly the car started to rock. Knowing we were parked on the edge of a gully, I opened my eyes to find the cause of the rocking. An elephant had his trunk in the open window and was rocking the car! We closed the window as soon as the elephant removed its trunk. First time I've been rocked to sleep by an elephant!"
>
> Peace Corps volunteer
> Togo

Let's follow Maria as she applies to the Peace Corps and starts her journey toward her goal of Peace Corps service.

- Maria recalls seeing a telephone number flash across the television screen in the Peace Corps ad, but she had been too sleepy to write it down. That number was 800-424-8580, the national Peace Corps recruiting number. When Maria looked up the Peace Corps in her telephone book, she found the number for the area office which serves Wisconsin. It is located in Minneapolis, Minnesota. She calls this number and asks for information on the Peace Corps and a volunteer application.

- After having read the materials that were

How to Become a Peace Corps Volunteer   55

sent to her about the Peace Corps, Maria fills out the volunteer application. It is nine pages of questions asking such things as name, address, work experience, education, and hobbies. It asks for eight "references"—people who know Maria and would be able to answer questions about whether she is right for the Peace Corps, and whether she will be a good volunteer. Maria also has to write down why she wants to be a volunteer. After much thought, Maria writes that she wants to travel, learn a new language, and help people who need a little extra assistance in order to have a good life.

• Maria mails in her application, and arranges for an interview with a Peace Corps recruiter at the

Agricultural projects are needed in Costa Rica as well as in many other countries. The Peace Corps usually finds every member of an American farming family qualified for service.

Minneapolis office. There are 17 area Peace Corps offices across the country. People who want to join the Peace Corps deal with these local offices, rather than with the national Peace Corps headquarters which is located in Washington, D.C. The recruiter asks Maria many questions. He is trying to decide whether Maria will be a good Peace Corps volunteer. Why does she want to join the Peace Corps? Will she be able to adjust to living in a different country? Will Maria be able to do the work and learn a new language? Does she get along with people and respect them? Does she have the skills needed for a Peace Corps assignment? Is she willing to give two years to the Peace Corps? Where does she want to serve? (Although prospective volunteers may express their preference for a certain country in which to serve, the final decision as to where they are assigned is made by the Peace Corps.)

• Maria waits anxiously to hear about her Peace Corps application. The references she listed are contacted and those people are asked questions about Maria. After checking more than 50 job assignments available in 60 countries, the Peace Corps staff in Washington, D.C., matches Maria's application with a job in Sudan, the largest country in Africa, located on the Red Sea. In Sudan, people use wood for cooking fires and for heat. So many people use wood that the forests in the northern part of the country have practically disappeared. Supplies of wood and charcoal must be transported from many miles away, and the prices have more than tripled in the past four years. Maria's job will be to write articles and edit pamphlets that will encourage the people of Sudan to cut down on their use of wood. She will be based in Khartoum, Sudan, working with Sudanese co-workers under a Sudanese supervisor. This job is perfect for Maria because of her experience editing the newsletter at the New Energy Woodstove Company. It is a good match.

- Maria is invited to be a Peace Corps volunteer. She joyfully accepts, and goes out to get a double banana split to celebrate. Even Mittens, her cat, celebrates with a new catnip ball, and they both spend a very happy evening.

"We were never at a loss for food. Almost every day someone would come by with food for us, and it was all good. We were sure to catch a few lobsters every day, and rounded out our diet with coconuts, bread fruit, and chickens raised by local farmers. All of this was eaten with our fingers, sitting on the floor. We refused, however, to try two of the local favorite foods—bat and pigeon!"

Peace Corps volunteer
Western Samoa

Trainees headed for Sudan learn to make a beehive stove in Evergreen, Colorado.

- Maria goes to the first official Peace Corps training program for her group of trainees assigned to Sudan. This training is held in Evergreen, Colorado. While Maria is there, she receives shots and has a physical examination. She and the other trainees receive instruction about the Sudanese culture, and many hours of Arabic language training. Maria also learns about layout and graphic design, which

Breaking up stone for the beehive stove which will help the Sundanese use their fuel more efficiently.

will help her in designing pamphlets in Sudan.
- Then Maria flies home for two days to say good-bye to her friends and family before she goes to Sudan. Everyone she knows is very excited, and one of her good friends gives a going-away party for her on her last night in Wauwatosa. Maria is happy, but sad also. She will not see her friends for a long time, and as she laughs and talks with them she tries to memorize their faces and voices, so she can remember them when she is in Sudan. Maria gives Mittens to her friends, the Ashbys, so she will know her cat is well taken care of while she is gone. She will fly to New York the next day, where she will leave for Sudan in Africa.
- Maria gets more training in Sudan. She continues learning Arabic, the language spoken there. Around the world, Peace Corps volunteers are taught the language spoken in the country they will serve. Over 75 different languages are taught by the Peace Corps. Maria is fortunate; in Sudan, some people also speak English. In addition to the language, Maria also learns about the history, religions, beliefs, and day-to-day skills needed to live in her new country.

Learning the ways of the people is important. In some Middle Eastern countries, Peace Corps volunteers learn that it is an insult to shake hands, touch someone, or offer gifts with the left hand. Peace Corps volunteers in areas of Latin America learn that single men and women may not go to any place together unless a third person, called a "chaperone," is with them. Learning these customs of the host country makes it easier to live and adjust during Peace Corps service.

Language lessons continue in the country where a volunteer serves.

• Maria Sanchez is now officially a Peace Corps volunteer and on the job. She is living in Khartoum, the capital of Sudan. Khartoum is on the Nile River, where the Blue Nile and the White Nile come together. It is a port city and a railway center. Maria will be in Sudan for the next two years.

Who could have imagined on that night so long ago, as Maria watched the late movie and almost slept through a Peace Corps ad, that a year later she would be halfway across the world serving the people of Sudan? Her dream had come true!

-6-
"Dear Mom and Dad and Timmy"

Most Peace Corps volunteers are anxious to share their experiences with their families. They write and receive lots of letters. Let's look at the kind of letters a typical Peace Corps volunteer might send home. Let's call this volunteer Terry Sykes. These are just some of the letters Terry might have written to his mother, father, and ten-year-old brother, Timmy, during two years of Peace Corps volunteer service in Zaire, Africa.

Dear Mom and Dad and Timmy,

When I got off the plane at Ndjili International Airport in Kinshasa, it was over 100 degrees! Kinshasa is a big city, larger than Philadelphia where Uncle Tony lives. There are a few high buildings, but the majority are overly crowded one-story cement houses. I was overwhelmed by the

Sign at the Bukavu Peace Corps training center

dilapidated conditions. So many people, and I couldn't understand anything they were saying!

I flew to Goma next, where I spent the night. I got my first taste of Zaire beer in Goma. The next morning I took a ferry across Lake Kivu to the city of Bukavu. A bus took me to this school for Peace Corps training before I begin my volunteer service.

Today is my third day of French language training. We can't speak English at the center! *Bonjour.* I will soon begin learning Tshiluba, another Zairian language. Actually, I think I'll end up speaking Tshiluba more than I'll speak French. I'm also learning about Zairian history and culture. Did you know that this country used to be the Belgian Congo? Or that it has large amounts of copper and diamonds?

Don't forget to number your letters. Then I'll know whether any are lost.

Terry

Dear Timmy,

I have been swimming in Lake Kivu every day during my lunch break. I can see high mountains rising in the distance from my window here at the Institut Superieur Pédagogique.

This week I went into Bukavu. The women were carrying a lot of things on their backs. They have really interesting hairstyles—very tight braids that stick straight out.

Women of Zaire have distinctive hairstyles.

The food is okay. I have to watch how much pepper I shake on everything because the pepper, *pili-pili*, is very hot. The bananas are only three inches long, but they taste like bananas back home in Texas, only sweeter.

Terry

Dear Mom and Dad,

I will be leaving soon for the village where I'll spend the next two years. It is Kakamba, in the Kazumba Zone, of the Kasai Occidental Region. This sounded complicated at first, until I realized how similar our method of pinpointing our homes in America is: League City, in the state of Texas, in the United States of America.

I was sworn into the Peace Corps yesterday. After ten weeks of technical training in Oklahoma, and ten weeks of language lessons here, I am now a real Peace Corps volunteer. My French is pretty good, and I can't wait to begin my work as a fish culture extension agent.

I miss following the Houston Rockets basketball team back in Texas. Soccer and tennis seem to be popular around here.

Terry

Dear Timmy,

My training told us what to expect in village life, and I'd been told about not having any electricity or running water. But being told and experiencing it are two different things!

Have you ever imagined what it would be like to be a fish in a fishbowl? I think I know. My biggest change so far in coming to Zaire is giving up my privacy. Villagers are always staring at me. They even look in my window to see what I'm doing. If I try to go off by myself to think, they assume I'm sick. Yesterday I went into the woods to get away from the children who were following me around. I wonder if I'll ever get used to this.

Terry

Dear Mom and Dad,

Thanks for the letter. You wanted to hear more about my living conditions. I live in a hut made

A village hut in Zaire— much larger than Terry's

of mud and stick walls with a thatched roof. It has two bedrooms and a living room. The whole building is only about 6 meters by 5 meters. I sleep on a palm frond framed bed, with a raffia mat. It's very firm, but comfortable. The dirt floor of the hut is kept smooth and clean by sprinkling water and sweeping the loose sand. I have no electricity, but use a kerosene lamp or candles to read at night. I have no refrigerator. Cooking is done in another tiny hut, and I eat outside.

There is no market in this village, so once or twice a week I travel four miles to one elsewhere in the zone—on my motorcycle! My closest encounter with a motorcycle in Texas was when one passed me on the highway. Now it's my only way to get around, besides walking. My motorcycle was given to me by the Agency for International Development (AID), since I am working on a Peace Corps/AID fish extension project.

Don't worry, though. I'm a good driver, and I wear my helmet. There's not much traffic on the dirt trails—mostly people walking. Some Zairians live all their lives without ever riding in a car. Some walk 30 miles to get to a market!

Terry

Dear Mom and Dad,

I'm sitting in my chair having a glass of palm wine, thinking of home. This wine tastes good. You can't buy it at a local store, like you would in America. You get palm wine by climbing a palm

Tapping a palm tree for palm wine. This one is in Cameroon.

70 THE PEACE CORPS TODAY

tree, making a cut in the bark, and setting squash gourds in place to catch the sap. This natural wine is then collected everyday in the afternoon, until the tree dies one to two months later.

Remember how I never wanted to try new foods, and you said that someday I'd realize that I couldn't eat hot dogs forever? That day has come! I don't think my new friends here can even imagine a hot dog.

Eating hasn't always been easy. I eat bananas, day after day, when I would rather be eating steak and potatoes. The availability of different foods is dependent on what is in season or being harvested.

A volunteer helps fish farmers in Kilembu, Zaire, to harvest a pond by seining.

But I'm getting used to all this. I've eaten grasshoppers, goat, and monkey meat.

I've even eaten flying ants! Catching the *nsua* (as they're called in Tshiluba) is a family affair. In November and December when the moon is full and rising on the horizon, the ants fly toward the light. So the Zairians dig a deep hole next to the ant mound, and place a candle at the bottom. The ants are fooled and fall into the hole, where they are scooped up and stuffed into a large bag to take back to the village for smoking, and then eaten or sold. A delicacy!

Terry

Dear Mom and Dad,

Preparing food for meals is a long process here. Women and girls spend a lot of time making manioc flour. First, the manioc root must be soaked for two days to get rid of the poisonous cyanide it contains. Then it must be dried, peeled, cut, pounded, and sifted into flour. This is done two times a day, and takes about thirty minutes each time! Manioc is used to make *bidia*. This is a paste, but kind of like bread dough. You eat it by taking pieces and dipping them in meat and vegetable dishes.

Women cook the food over outside fires. On hot days this seems almost unbearable. Women also tend the crops, do the marketing, carry water and firewood, and other backbreaking jobs.

I get Z4000 a month (around $100) from the Peace Corps as a living allowance. It probably doesn't seem like much money, but around here it is a lot. Zaires are this country's form of money.

The paper money has a picture of the President of Zaire on one side, and the national flag on the other. I buy salted fish and fresh meat at the market. I cook the meat and eat it later, because I can't refrigerate it.

The Zairian boys here add to their families' dinners with the rodents and birds they get with their slingshots. Every boy has a slingshot.

             Terry

Dear Mom and Dad,

I have been telling my teenage friend Mulumba a little about my home. When I can't think of the correct word in the Tshiluba language, I switch to French.

My work is going well. I get up at dawn, and spend most of the day traveling by motorcycle to visit farmers in the area. I work with them to build and maintain fish ponds. The people here don't get enough protein to eat, but I'm trying to help the farmers realize that fish ponds can bring them more than just food; fish can bring extra money. If the only purpose was to raise fish to eat, the ponds would probably be abandoned after I return to Texas. The important thing I emphasize is "fish for profit."

First we select the site for the pond at the bottom of the valley. Once the pond is built, I bring fingerlings, small fish that the farmer buys from another established fish farmer, to stock the pond. Two

Sometimes a pond is drained and the fish collected. Fish pond projects in Zaire . . .

74   THE PEACE CORPS TODAY

. . . help the local farmers to raise fish for food and for profit.

compost fences in each pond provide nutrients in the water and support the growth of algae and plankton for the fish to eat. I drop in on two to four farmers each day. I enjoy the meals I share with them, and the discussions we have. We talk about a lot of things, and have a great time.

Terry

Dear Mom and Dad,
"House-husbands" are not a new thing here. The men of the village always watch the younger children while the women work in the fields.

An interesting thing happened last night. A neighbor, Kabasele, slept in my extra bedroom because he complained that there were spirits in his room! Although most of the villagers are Catholic, many still believe in evil spirits. This morning another neighbor put some charms in Kabasele's hut to ward off the evil spirits. They were locks of hair with chicken bones.

Enjoyed seeing other Peace Corps volunteers at a recent meeting in Kinshasa of all the Peace Corps volunteers working on fish projects. It was good to get away and relax, but after a few days I was eager to return home to my hut here in Kakamba.

Terry

Dear Mom and Dad,
Sometimes I think I would go crazy if it wasn't for my radio. I listen to the Voice of America broadcasts. I spent at least an hour last night thinking how great it would be to hear a real live person speak English. I began to worry I'd forgotten how to speak English, so I started talking to myself. If you'd been here, you would have thought that I *did* go crazy.

I get lonely every now and then. In the United States, there would be so much to do, and things wouldn't be so frustrating. But people everywhere have problems, and the villagers here are so friendly to me. They react to my presence with curiosity and wonderment. My neighbors bring me gifts, and ask me about my home across the ocean. I've told them a little about you. On the whole, I'd have to say I was happy here in Zaire.

               Terry

Dear Timmy,
 The names here confused me at first. I can't tell from the name whether the person is a boy or girl. (I guess you could say the same thing about my name, Terry!). I've previously mentioned my friends Mulumba and Kabasele. Other good friends are Kapinga and Mbombo. Mulumba has twin sisters named Konku and Mbuyi. There is another set of twins here in Kakamba, two boys, also named Konku and Mbuyi. I guess those are the favored names for all twins born here.
 You wonder what children like you do all day? This is a typical day for a young boy in Kakamba.
 Breakfast would probably be leftover *bidia* (manioc/corn paste) with *matamba* (pounded manioc leaves). His schoolday begins at 8:00 A.M. The classrooms, one for each grade, are made by the previous class's students. Sticks are lashed together for walls; the students sit in rows on a long, thick stick, elevated by two other sticks driven into

A group of children in Zaire

the ground. He would learn French, math, basic science, and writing. School only lasts until noon. The afternoon is spent in the woods with his slingshot, or working with his mother in the field. He enjoys playing marbles, and soccer. The boys usually kick a tightly wound wad of paper, because they can't afford a regular ball. I bought a rubber ball for my neighbor boys, and they continued to use it even after it was punctured! Kakamba boys carve trucks from balsa wood. Evening might find them racing back and forth through the village singing chants. But they also love dancing to the sounds of a "band"—villagers playing xylophones, drums, and a bottle tapped with a spoon. Bedtime comes early because it gets dark quickly and there are no electric lights.

Terry

Dear Mom and Dad and Timmy,

I miss you. While you're feasting on Thanksgiving turkey and pumpkin pie, I have to settle for *bidia* and *matamba*. You'll be watching the football game and parades. I'll be counting fish in a pond.

But I may drink some palm wine tonight with my friends. We may have as much excitement as we did last week. There was a huge storm (rainy season here is from September to April), and the villagers thought it was caused by the chief of the Kazumba Zone. The women of the village jogged to the chief's house—singing, chanting, and waving leaves and hoes to protest the storm. As providers for their families, it falls upon the women to handle natural disasters. Quite a sight!

Enjoy your meal, and I will enjoy mine.

Terry

Dear Mom and Dad,

A baby was born here last week. She died today. There are a lot of childhood diseases in Kakamba. Mothers have ten children, and sometimes as many as five will die. People don't live very long in Zaire. Life expectancy is forty-five for a man. It's sad to realize this.

I have come to love my friends here. These people mean something to me which I have never felt before. It's hard to explain. They learn from me, I learn from them. But it's not easy. I no longer expect a lot. If I could just change the farmers' thought processes a bit, so that instead of always thinking just of today, they can picture tomorrow. I realize I feel low when nothing goes right. But I
have found I can get through it. I really look forward to the rest of my time in Zaire.

Terry

Dear Mom and Dad,

My Peace Corps volunteer service will soon be completed. Last year I was counting the days until I could leave. I seemed to be having no impact on the lives of the people here. What have I actually accomplished? Some fish ponds have been built. That doesn't sound like much. But when I've been down, I've remembered that I'll be followed by another Peace Corps volunteer, and another Peace Corps volunteer will follow that one. By the time the son of a farmer with whom I work grows up, he

80　*THE PEACE CORPS TODAY*

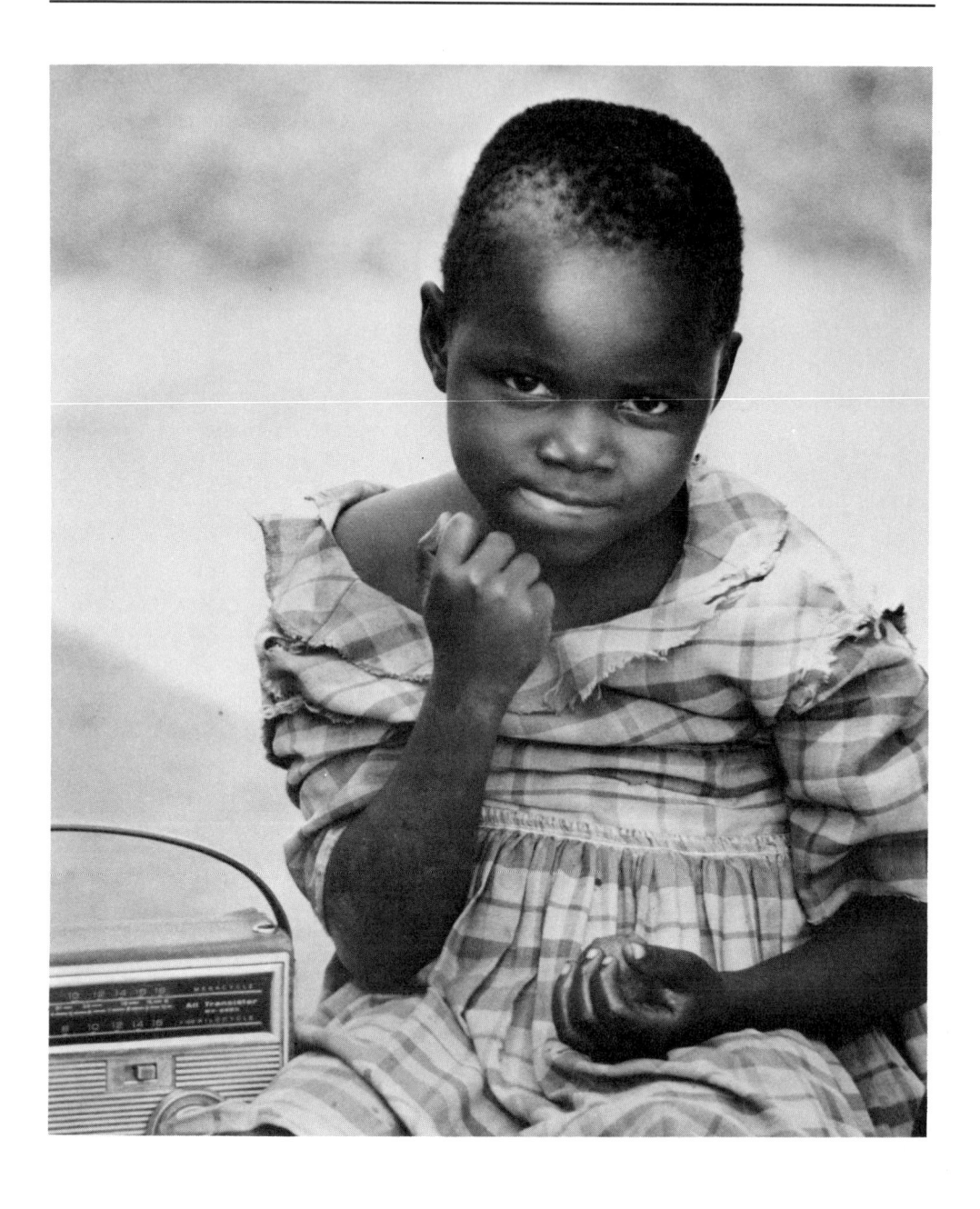

may see that fish can be profitable, and that our advice does work. Some day, our work may make a difference.

Terry

Dear Mom and Dad,

I will be stopping a few places here before I return home. I want to go to the Virunga National Park in Zaire, visit Kenya, and spend more time in Paris. You know, Africa is not at all like the Tarzan movies we used to watch. There are so many different countries in Africa. It is such a diverse, culturally rich continent, yet in many places the people are so poor and malnourished.

I bet it will probably take me a while to get used to the fast pace of American life again. The intense heat here makes everyone slow down. Texas summers will seem almost cool! I like knowing everyone here and being an important person in my village. When I return home I will be a nobody again. I don't even know everyone in our immediate neighborhood there.

I want to leave, yet I want to stay. I have made such good friends, and I'll probably never see them again. I will miss them. I would like to have done more. I regret all I haven't accomplished. But I also want to get on with my own life.

I joined the Peace Corps to travel, learn another language, and to help other people. I've faced a great challenge in the past two years, and have become a

Opposite page: Little Zairian girl with a radio

stronger person because of it. I don't think I'll ever take water, electricity, or food for granted again. I don't think I'll ever be the same person I was.

The Zairians, although poorer than Americans, are richer in many ways. There's a great deal of beauty in their simplicity.

So air out my old bedroom, stock up on peanut butter and hot dogs. I'm coming home!

Terry

-7-
Returned Peace Corps Volunteers

What do a United States Senator, the President of a National Football League team, the inventor of the "Snugli" infant carrier, and a designer of creative playgrounds have in common? All four of these people are returned Peace Corps volunteers.

What happens to Peace Corps volunteers after their service is over? Most Peace Corps volunteers return to their homes in America when their volunteer time is finished. Once home, they can again enjoy hot baths, refrigerators, and television. Over 100,000 returned Peace Corps volunteers are here living among us right now.

Returned Peace Corps volunteers look like your teacher, the president of the bank down the street, and the person on the local television news program. They hold all kinds of jobs, and resemble other Americans.

But they are not the same. Returned Peace Corps

volunteers have shared the experience of living and working in another culture, representing America to the people there, and they will forever be different because of it.

These technical skills, knowledge of foreign languages, and understanding of other people and places that returned Peace Corps volunteers bring back with them can be given to America upon their return home.

This effect on our country was predicted by the first Director of the Peace Corps, Sargent Shriver.

"Probably the most important development in

Paul Tsongas and Christopher Dodd were both Peace Corps volunteers before becoming members of the House of Representatives and later the Senate.

the future of the Peace Corps will be the impact of returning volunteers on American society," he said in a speech given in October, 1965. "Before long five thousand Peace Corps volunteers a year will be returning from having lived and worked overseas, under difficult conditions, among strange cultures, lands, and people. They will be a new breed of Americans."

This new breed of Americans often shares its experiences, teaching people in America about life in countries very far from home. But it is not always easy.

"My students were mostly of Indian ancestry, with a few native Fijians. They expected strict discipline in the classroom, standing at attention beside their desks when a 'Master' entered. They enjoyed new experiences, especially doing science experiments themselves. During an open house, I set up several experiments in the chemistry lab as demonstrations. One was the Goldschmidt reaction for making molten iron. It is quite a spectacular fireworks display, but on the first try, the fuse went out. A second try was much more vigorous than expected, and showered the school board members, the principal, my students, and me with a white powder of aluminum oxide!"

Peace Corps volunteer
Fiji

Sometimes it is hard to readjust to life there, after being out of the country for several years.

"People can't relate to what you've done, you can't relate to them," said one returned Peace Corps volunteer. As a result of service, some returned Peace Corps volunteers feel that Americans don't need most of the possessions they have.

"I don't need as much stuff now," said a returned Peace Corps volunteer who served in Togo. "I saw people get by on a lot less. It makes life a lot simpler."

Often, the returned Peace Corps volunteer must get used to a quicker life-style again, much different from the slow pace in the village where he or she lived for the past two years.

In an attempt to meet these special needs of returned Peace Corps volunteers, and make reentry into American life easier for them, the National Council of Returned Peace Corps Volunteers was formed in 1979. There are also many local groups for returned Peace Corps volunteers in cities all across the United States. These groups have two main goals: to help the returned volunteer readjust to life in the U.S. through the help of other returned volunteers, and to "help promote a better understanding of other peoples on the part of the American people," which is the Peace Corps' third goal.

"The benefits of the Peace Corps will not be limited to the countries where it serves," said President John F. Kennedy in 1961. "Our own young men

Opposite page: Christopher Dodd during Peace Corps training in Puerto Rico

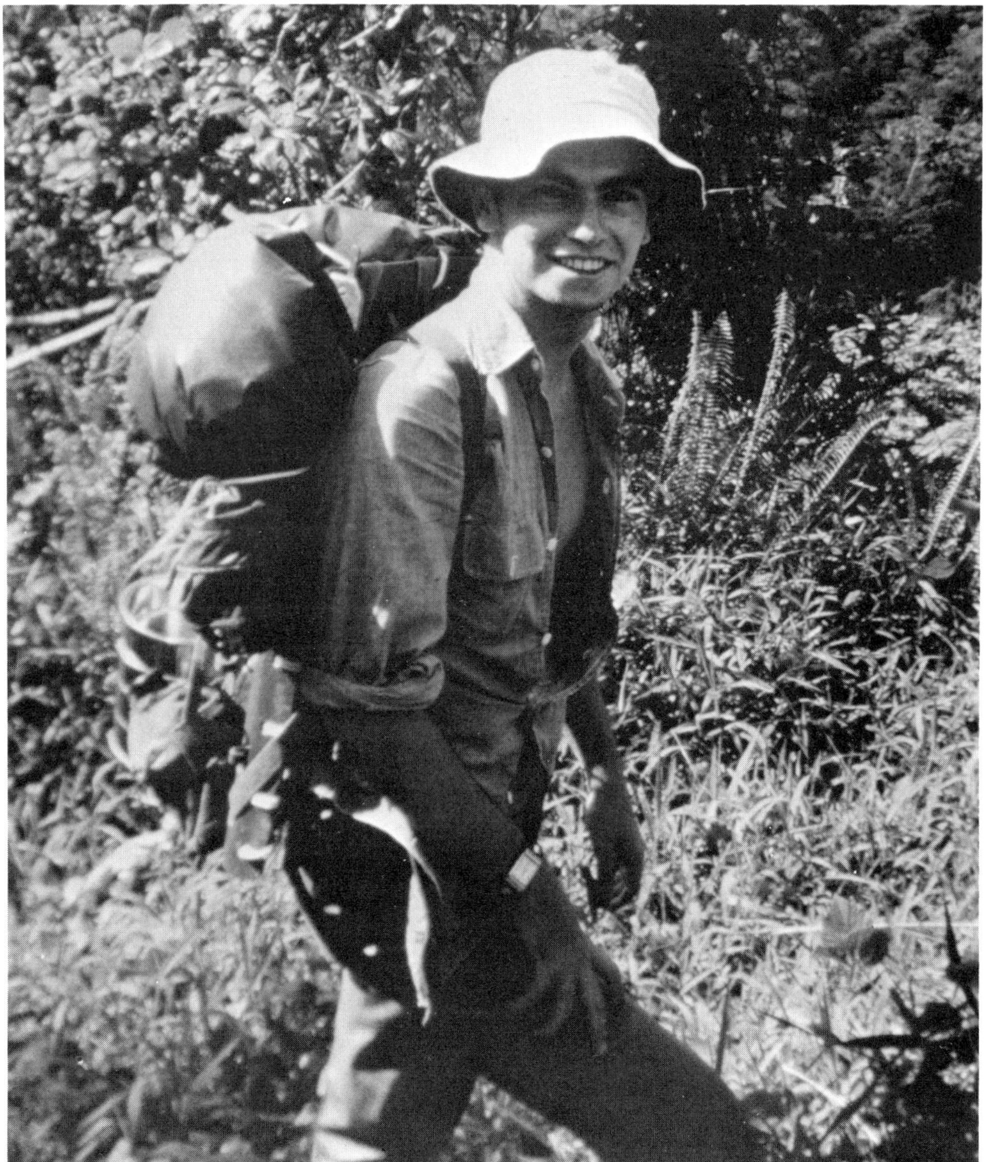

and women will be enriched by the experience of living and working in foreign lands. They will have acquired new skills and experience which will aid them in their future careers, and add to our own country's supply of trained personnel and teachers."

> "Children everywhere like to play tricks on teachers, and see them get upset. Today I was lecturing and writing on the board and heard some snickers in the class. Two inches from my hand was a creeping scorpion. They were awaiting the sting with grinning anticipation."
>
> Peace Corps volunteer
> Kenya

Many returned Peace Corps volunteers serve in the Foreign Service. They have also become Congressmen, ambassadors, lawyers, and hospital administrators. They look back on their Peace Corps service as being invaluable training for their present jobs.

Some returned Peace Corps volunteers can return from service to talk over their experiences with another returned volunteer in their own family. In one family, a mother finally joined the Peace Corps herself after having waved good-bye to a son and daughter-in-law who became volunteers ten years

Opposite page: Paul Tsongas talks with students in Ethiopia where he served as a Peace Corps volunteer.

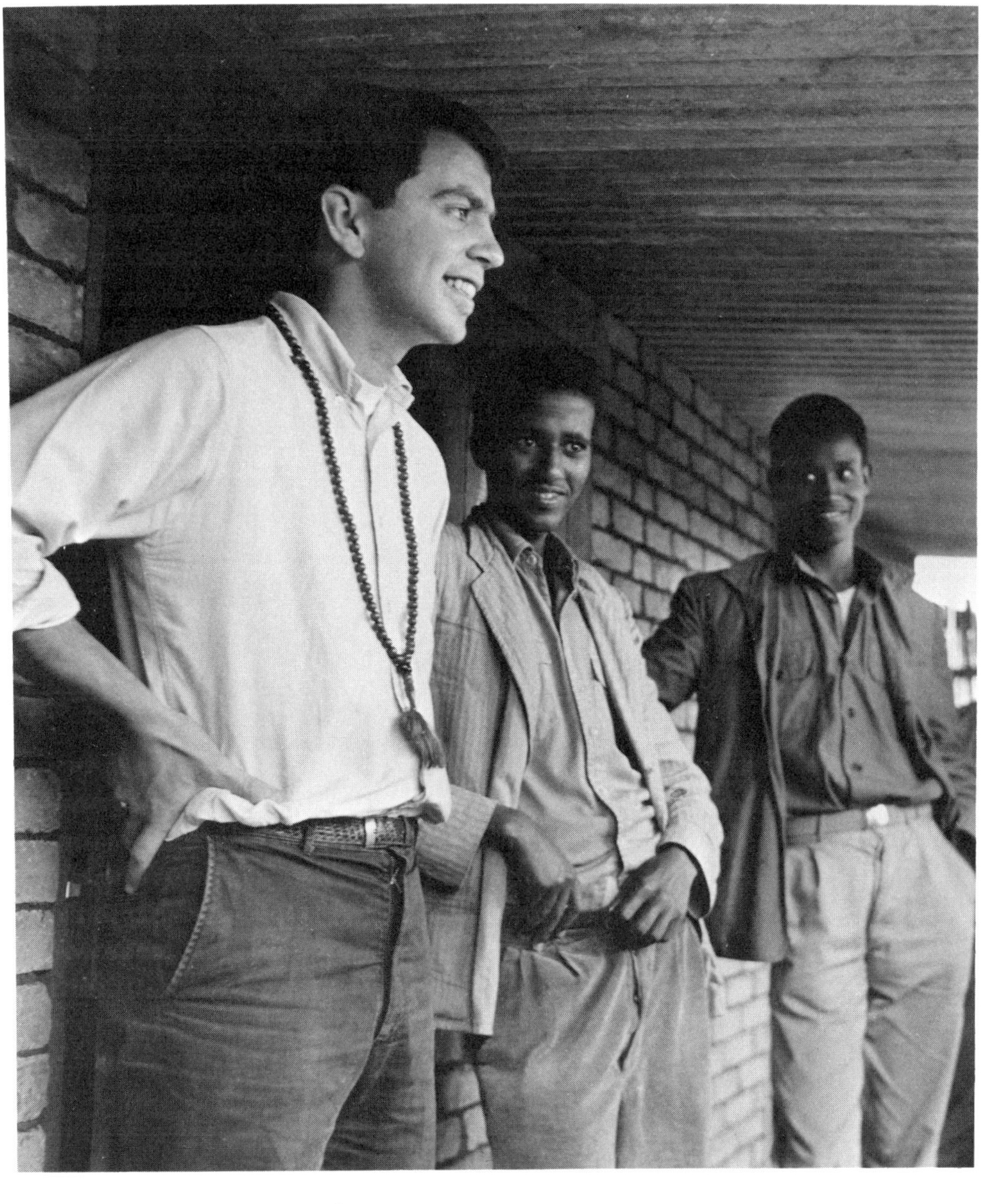

before, and another son and daughter-in-law who had been Peace Corps volunteers before them. Peace Corps service spanned three generations in another family. The father served as a volunteer in Malaysia, his daughter served in Turkey, and his granddaughter served in Western Samoa.

Returned Peace Corps volunteers will always have certain things in common. They share memories, an outlook on life gained from firsthand knowledge of a different culture, and an understanding of people from different backgrounds. As one returned volunteer from Chile described it: "We might be strangers when we meet, and yet one returned Peace Corps volunteer will instantly feel a bond with another."

-8-
It's a Small World

Have you ever wondered what children are like in different countries around the world? What do they eat, what do they wear, what do they play with? Peace Corps volunteers get to know the children in other countries where they serve. Some volunteers know them from the schools or clinics where they work; other volunteers know the children as neighbors and friends. Let's meet some of these young people.

Rowena lives in the Philippines. Her country of over 7,000 islands is located in the Pacific Ocean, halfway around the world from the United States. Rowena spends most of her daytime hours in school. She awakens early, in order to arrive there by 8:00 A.M. Like all the Filipino children in her village, she wears thonged rubber sandals. Because everyone walks barefoot inside buildings, the children slip

92   THE PEACE CORPS TODAY

their sandals off at the doorways, and just as easily slip them back on when leaving.

Rowena and her friends walk arm in arm to their school. When they arrive, Rowena notices that her teacher is wearing green. Immediately she knows that it is Wednesday. How does she know that? You can tell what day of the week it is by looking at the teachers' clothes. Teachers wear uniforms three days of the week, a different color for each of the days. They wear their own clothing the other two days. So, if Rowena's teacher is wearing a green uniform, everyone knows it is Wednesday.

Opposite page: Children of the Philippines

Below: A classroom in the Philippines

During part of the morning, Rowena works in the gardens, tending crops that will be sold to make money for her school. Soon it is lunchtime, and Rowena starts home for her meal. She and her friends look forward to being sixth graders, because they are allowed to stay at school during lunchtime and cook meals for their teachers. But Rowena enjoys going home at midday, since it gives her a chance to say hello to her friend, Vincent Carter. Vincent is a Peace Corps volunteer who works at the clinic located between the school and Rowena's house. He gave Rowena a vaccination shot last year, and was so gentle and kind during her visit that they became good friends. Rowena only stays a minute at the clinic, so she will not be late for lunch.

> **"I lived in a boarding house in a small town in Korea. The house was in a compound with walls around it. My room was on a corner, so I had two windows facing out over the fields. All the kids in town would play right outside and when one got brave he would climb the wall to look in and watch the American. When they finally did visit me, the kids loved to feel the hair on my arms, and one asked if I could really see with blue eyes!"**
>
> **Peace Corps volunteer
> Korea**

The Truk Islands are part of the Eastern Caroline Islands, located east of the Philippines in the Pacific Ocean. John is a sixth grader there. When his teacher, Abe May, was introduced at the beginning of the year, John studied him carefully. He was in awe of the blond, blue-eyed American, who explained that he was a Peace Corps volunteer. After awhile, John grew used to Mr. May and put extra effort into his schoolwork in order to please him.

John really worked hard on one particular project. It was a report on turtles, or *pwapwa* as they are called in the Trukese language. The report described the hunting, preparing, and cooking of turtles, one of the tastiest meats served in the Truk Islands. John wrote that the chief has the supreme authority to decide when to kill the turtles, and how the meat is to be divided. The other parts of the turtles are also used. Children use the gallbladder as a balloon. Turtle shells are made into combs, jewelry, fishhooks, and plates. Turtle bones are used for decorations and weaving needles.

After reading John's report about turtles, Mr. May complimented him for the fine job he had done, and admitted that he had not had much experience with turtles. John was pleased, and invited Mr. May for dinner the next time they were having turtle meat.

Children in Villarrica, Paraguay, a country in

Teaching boys in Paraguay

South America, speak Spanish. They go to school for half a day, either the morning session from 7:00 to 11:30 A.M. or the afternoon one from 1:00 to 5:30 P.M. The school day begins with everyone lined up in front of the building, singing their national anthem. Children wear uniforms of white blouses, blue skirts or shorts, and white jackets. Some children don't wear shoes; many do not have books to use. During recess the boys play soccer and marbles, while the girls play with jacks or jump rope. Many children in Paraguay leave school at the age of ten or eleven to become apprentices. They live with a skilled adult and slowly learn their trade or craft. By the time they are seventeen or eighteen, the youngsters have the knowledge and ability to work as craftsmen.

A Peace Corps volunteer in the Central African Republic was talking with some children in his village. They couldn't believe that there were no mango trees in American cities. All villages in the Central African Republic have mango trees, and they are one of the only sources of food from May to June. One child asked, "If there are no mango trees, what do you eat at the end of the dry season?"

The children in the Central African Republic make toys from wire and old cans. These toys look like cars or trucks, and the youngsters spend many hours "driving" them around their village.

> "The noise was puzzling. Having awakened from a sound sleep, I heard a very strange sound. Screeching, almost laughing, came from outside my hut, which was located at the far end of my village in the Central African Republic. The sound continued, and as I sat listening I tried to get the courage to investigate. Finally convincing myself of the importance of finding out the source of the noises, I walked quietly across the room and slowly opened the door. I carefully stuck my head out, and discovered several hyenas eating the front seats out of my jeep. Noting their number and apparent appetite, I softly wished them 'good night,' and returned to my bed and slumber."
>
> Peace Corps volunteer
> Central African Republic

Opposite page: Schoolchildren in Ecuador assist a volunteer to grow vegetables on land that surrounds public schools.

Eugene Boahene is a thirteen-year-old boy who lives in Ghana in Africa. He enjoys eating, and so he wrote about his favorite foods in a report for his Peace Corps teacher.

"There are so many delicious types of dishes in Ghana. Some of the foods are porridge, and others are made from food crops. *Koko* and rice-water are some traditional porridges. *Koko* is made from corn dough mixed with water and cooked. Sugar can be added to taste. Rice-water is cooked rice mixed with sugar. Some other foods are *fufu, ampesi, banku,* rice-balls, *akple, kokonle,* and *kpekple.* Out of all of these,

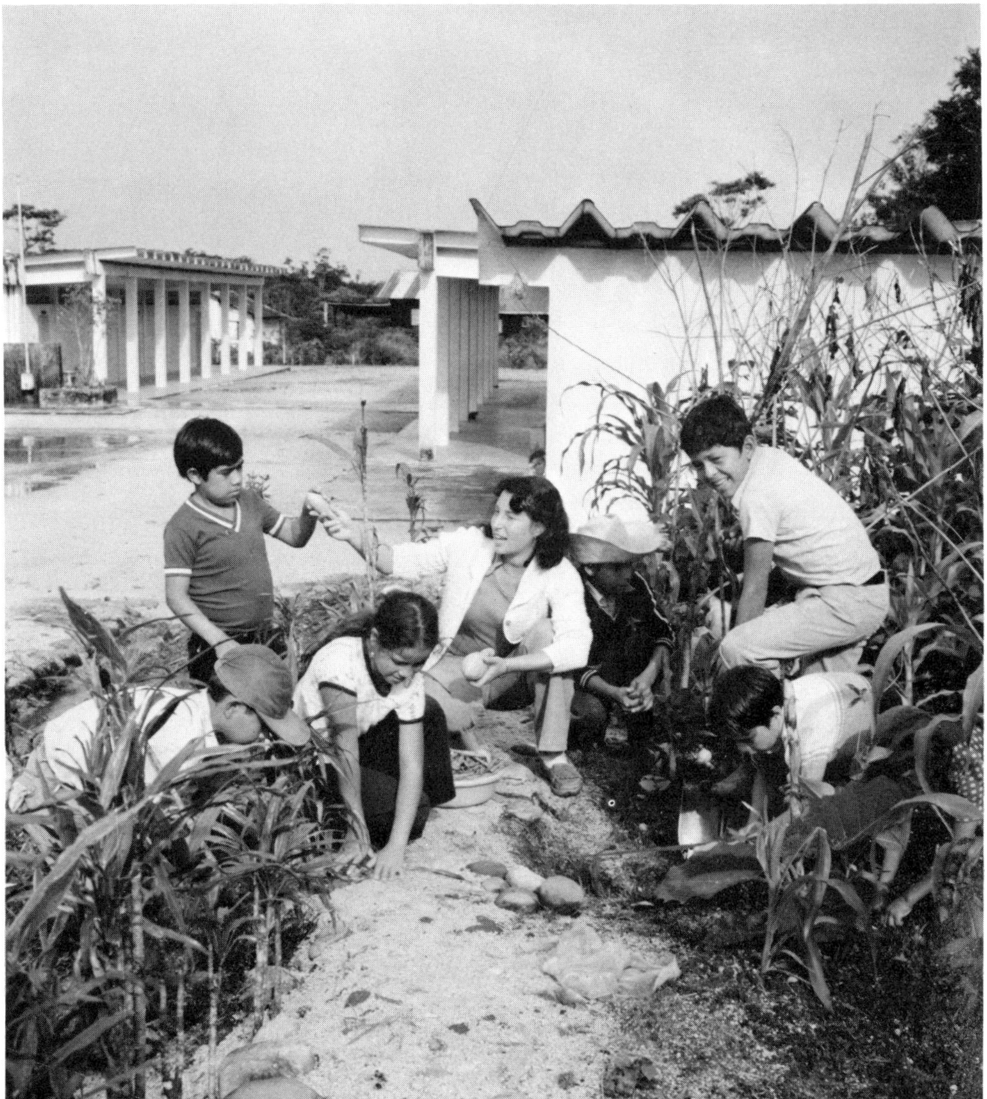

fufu is the most popular. It is made of either cocoyam, plantain, cassava, or yam. These must be peeled and cooked, then pounded in a mortar. *Fufu* can be served with soups such as groundnut or palma-nut."

A Peace Corps volunteer in Honduras, a country in Central America, describes the children there.

Likes: Sweet popsicles, loud disco music, piñata parties for birthdays.

Dress: Always uniforms for school.

School: Lots of chanting and memory work. Children often sit two to a desk because there are not enough desks.

Activities: Many small towns have electricity only for three to four hours in the evening, so children gather at a neighbor's house to watch television, no matter what show is on. All children jump rope. All children like to sing nonsense songs. Boys play soccer.

Work: Grinding corn for tortillas, carrying water, washing clothes, and caring for younger brothers and sisters.

Peace Corps volunteers discover that even though everyone in the world doesn't speak the same language, or have the same things—television, toys, books—deep down inside people are pretty much alike. They find that everyone doesn't think the same way or act the same way, that there are often

Opposite page: Child in Togo playing with an old bicycle rim

It's a Small World 101

no right or wrong ways of doing things, but many different ways. Yet children in Paraguay, the Philippines, Kenya, and America have similar needs: they want to have fun with their friends, have clothes to wear, and food to eat. They want to be an important part of their family.

You may have heard the expression, "It's a small world." Peace Corps volunteers know what this means: the world is made up of people who are different yet share the same basic feelings. By building bridges of understanding and friendship, they help make this a small world.

-9-
Peace Corps Partnership Program

Imagine a dry, scorching day, a day so hot it is 95 degrees in the shade. You are walking to school. Every step you take kicks dust from the dirt road into your face and mouth. You finally arrive at school, two hours after leaving home, and rush to get a drink of water to relieve your parched throat. But there is no water.

Luckily, this experience may never happen to you. It had never happened to Girl Scout Troops 1081 and 860 of Westminster, Colorado. How, then, did they get involved with the students of Shri Siddha Prithibi Janta Vocational High School in Nepal, a country bordering India where this scene occured every morning?

Angelita laughed in delight as she watched the antics of the colorful puppets. When the puppet show was over, she sang some songs and colored a picture with her crayons. The week before, two adults wearing white clown makeup, dark clothes, and colorful suspenders had done a pantomine skit for Angelita's primary school class in the South American country of Ecuador. Angelita enjoyed the puppets, music, art, and mime. But more importantly, Angelita now knows how important it is to drink lots of milk.

What does milk have to do with puppets and mime? How did the students at Urey Middle School in Walkerton, Indiana, get involved with Angelita, puppets, and milk in Ecuador?

The answer to both questions is the Peace Corps Partnership Program. This program helps people in other countries by transmitting money from schools, churches, clubs, and businesses in the United States to communities overseas for projects that will improve their lives. It also promotes international friendship by making possible personal exchanges, such as letters, books, and toys, between the overseas and U.S. partners.

At the Shri Siddha Prithibi Janta Vocational High School in Sriguan, Nepal, the water situation was very serious. In hot weather the nearest water was over a mile away in a small stream. Three custodians had to carry water in garden cans back and forth from the stream all day so that there was enough water for the 800 students.

The headmaster and teachers at the Nepalese high school wanted to solve their water problem by

This volunteer in Nepal dresses in the local fashion.

building a well and water pump. Besides making drinking water available to students, a clean source of water would enable the school to plant a fruit orchard on the extra school land, and increase the vocational classes taught at the school.

A Peace Corps volunteer, who teaches math and science at the high school, wrote a letter to the Peace Corps Partnership Program outlining the plans to build a well and water pump, and requesting help.

Meanwhile, in Westminster, Colorado, a suburb of Denver, the Girl Scouts in Troops 1081 and 860 were making plans to spend their hard-earned Girl Scout cookie profits. The twenty girls, in grades four to eight, chose to become Peace Corps Partners with the people of Sriguan and donate their money to the well project in Nepal.

A well in Nepal

"The girls felt that since water was a basic necessity of life, they wanted to help the Nepalese students get enough water," remembers their Girl Scout leader. "So they chose to support the Peace Corps Partnership Program, from among the many possible uses for their funds. It gave the girls a sense of perspective. Even as children they could do something to help their Nepalese neighbors half a world away."

The high school in Nepal received a new well and water pump, and the Girl Scouts began a lasting friendship with the community of Srigaun, Nepal.

"My husband and I left our grass hut and walked to the school where we would teach the children about health. The children were Bri Bri Indians, who sometimes went to school barefoot, carrying one notebook that would last them the whole school year, and one pencil that would be shared by the whole family. I remembered as a child getting carried away at the pencil sharpener, diligently sharpening the pencil until it was only inches long. No waste like that here, I thought. The children here aren't as lucky as we were, but they still seem totally happy! An interesting thought to consider, I reflected, as I entered the grass school building in the middle of the jungle in Costa Rica."

**Peace Corps volunteer
Costa Rica**

Children in Ecuador learn the proper way of brushing their teeth.

In Ecuador, many children have health problems because of their diet, despite the best efforts of the Ecuadorian people. Because of a lack of calcium, found in milk and green leafy vegetables, some children do not have strong bones and teeth. Many children do not understand what a proper diet is.

Two Peace Corps volunteers wanted to change this. With the support of teachers and parents, they developed a program featuring puppets, pantomine, drama, music, and dance that makes nutrition (the study of diet and health) come alive for the children in primary schools in Ecuador. Angelita learned about drinking milk through this nutrition education program.

But where would the volunteers get the money to bring this program to other children in Ecuador?

The Peace Corps Partnership Program was contacted by the two Peace Corps volunteers, and help was requested for the nutrition education program.

The Urey Middle School in Walkerton, Indiana, donated the money needed for the teaching program designed for first to sixth graders in the Ecuadorian provinces of Azvay and Manabi. Hopefully, this program will spread to other schools across Ecuador. The Middle School students in America became Peace Corps Partners with the primary school students in Ecuador.

Many other groups in America have become Peace Corps Partners with people around the world.

The first graders of Mann School in Oak Park, Illinois, are Peace Corps Partners with the kindergarteners in San Jeronimo, Honduras. The Oak Park children wrote letters to their new friends in Honduras, and sent them three big boxes filled with items that represent their lives in Oak Park, Illinois. The boxes contained balloons, ''scratch and sniff'' stick-

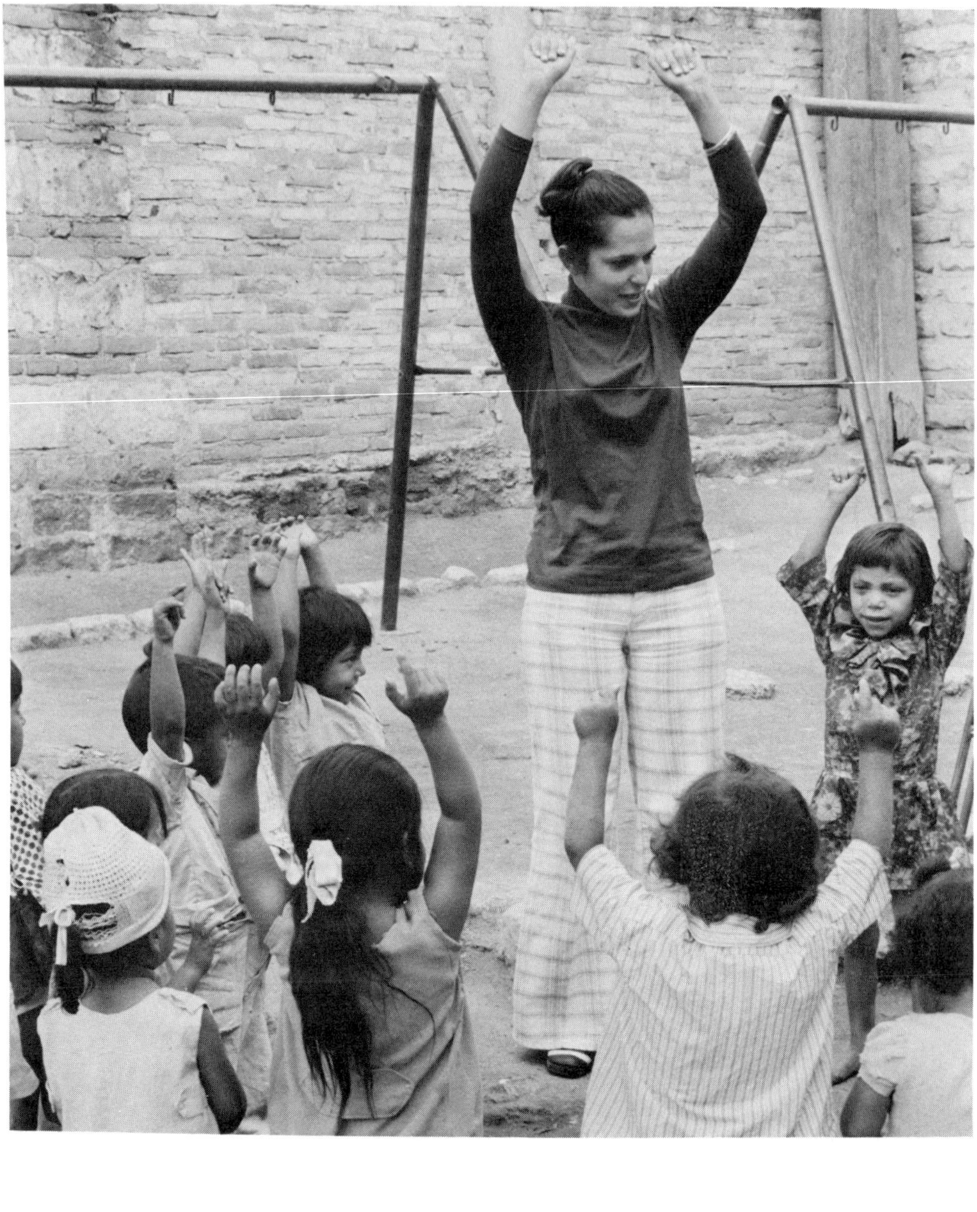

ers, bubble gum, crayons, jump ropes, kites, a kaleidoscope, and many other things.

> "The children in Malaysia are particularly keen on sports. The main ones are football (soccer to Americans) and *sepak takraw*, which is a game similar to volleyball but is played with a woven rattan ball which can only be hit with your feet or your head as in soccer. They are also keen on watching television, in particular a Japanese cartoon called 'Ultraman,' and an Arabian cartoon called 'Ali Baba,' both of which are translated into Malay."
>
> Peace Corps volunteer
> Malaysia

The newspaper vendors in Cabanas, Honduras, are learning a new trade in a sewing program at the local community center, thanks to their Peace Corps Partners, the Sioux City Boys Club of Iowa.

The Peace Corps Partnership Program has been helping our international neighbors and friends for over twenty years. In each project, the American partners discover that countries halfway around the world are really very close to home.

If you or a group you belong to would like to become Peace Corps Partners with youngsters in an-

Opposite page: Youngsters in Honduras with their Peace Corps teacher

other country, you can find out about the program by contacting:

    Peace Corps Partnership Program
    806 Connecticut Avenue, N.W.,
    Room M-1210
    Washington, D.C. 20526

Or call, toll free: 1-800-424-8580, ext. 227

-10-
How YOU Can Help the Peace Corps

Since the birth of the Peace Corps, young people across America have wanted to get involved with its programs. Enthusiasm for the Peace Corps does not have to wait until you are eighteen, the minimum age for applying to be a Peace Corps volunteer.

There are steps you can take *now* to prepare for future Peace Corps service. There are also ways to help promote the goals of international peace and friendship, even though it may be years before you can help people by becoming a volunteer.

One or more of the following activities may interest you. Addresses for organizations are given, in case you want to contact them for further information.

Travel or Study Abroad

Traveling with your family or friends is fun, and can also be a valuable learning experience. Just traveling to a distant relative's home or to summer camp

Opposite page: Young people in other countries, such as Costa Rica, like many of the same things you do.

can help your future Peace Corps service because you will learn how to prepare for travel—the correct way to pack your clothes and belongings, how to get around in a place many miles from home. Journeying to another country (if you are lucky enough to get the chance!) means that you will find out how to obtain a passport, what shots are necessary, how to communicate if they don't speak your language in the country you visit.

Student Exchange Programs further international understanding on a one-to-one basis. They are primarily for high school students, and are excellent opportunities when you reach fifteen to nineteen years of age. Generally, students live abroad with a host family, going to the local schools and meeting new friends. Programs vary in length from several weeks to a year. Some programs offer scholarships that give you financial assistance for your stay. An example is the Youth for Understanding/Peace Corps Scholarship Program, for students who have been nominated by Peace Corps volunteers or returned Peace Corps volunteers. Information about this program can be obtained by writing:

Youth for Understanding
International Student Exchange
3501 Newark Street, N.W.
Washington, D.C. 20016

A booklet entitled "One Friendship at a Time: Your Guide to International Youth Exchange" con-

How You Can Help the Peace Corps 115

tains information about approximately thirty organizations that offer international youth exchange programs of varying kinds. The booklet can be obtained free of charge by writing to either of these addresses:

President's International Youth Exchange
Pueblo, Colorado 81009

The U.S. Information Agency
Youth Exchange Staff
400 C Street, N.W.
Washington, D.C. 20547

Other addresses for information about exchange programs (including those for persons with disabilities from Mobility International) are:

Friendship Force International
575 S. Omni International
Atlanta, Georgia 30303

Foster Parents Plan/High School International Education Program
155 Plan Way
Warwick, Rhode Island 02887

Mobility International, USA
Box 3551
Eugene, Oregon 97402

Children's International Summer Villages give eleven-year-olds a chance to travel to other countries and attend a four-week international summer camp. The boys and girls meet children from other countries while living together at the camp and sharing games, food, and experiences.

    Children's International Summer Villages, Inc.
    USA National Office
    206 North Main Street, Box YX
    Casstown, Ohio 45312

The Girl Scouts offer International Wider Opportunities for older girls (Cadettes and Seniors). The girls travel to countries around the world to participate in programs planned by the local Girl Scouts and Girl Guides. Besides learning new skills, girls often work together on service projects designed to help people in the sponsoring country.

    Girl Scouts of the USA
    830 Third Avenue
    New York, N.Y. 10022

Participation in sports competition in other countries is possible. There will be an Olympic Youth Camp at future Olympic games for youth from Olympic countries to meet and share a week together. There are also sports for the handicapped, and Sport for Understanding teams up young people

118   THE PEACE CORPS TODAY

Opposite page: This volunteer was fluent in Vietnamese before learning Swahili, the language used in Kenya.

from all over the country to live and practice their favorite sport for one month in another land. Some of the events are backpacking, basketball, baseball, gymnastics, soccer, and swimming.

AAU/USA Junior Olympics
3400 W. 86th Street
Indianapolis, Indiana 46268

National Handicapped Sports and Recreation Association
P.O. Box 33141
Farragut Station
Washington, D.C. 20033

Below: This volunteer works with learning disabled students in a sports program in Ecuador.

Sport for Understanding
35001 Newark Street, N.W.
Washington, D.C. 20016

Study Foreign Languages and Cultures

Peace Corps volunteers must learn the language spoken in the area they plan to serve. Previous knowledge of a foreign language is helpful. Although that particular language may not be needed for your future Peace Corps assignment, the discipline and concentration you develop while learning it will help you in other foreign language studies.

Peace Corps volunteers always learn about the culture of the country they will serve. Taking world culture and world geography classes in school will help you learn about other countries and become familiar with their customs, food, and artifacts. Save the Children Federation offers exhibits, speakers, and other programs designed to get you directly involved in writing and thinking about other children around the world.

> Save the Children Federation, Inc.
> 54 Wilton Road
> Westport, Connecticut 06880

Your local library has many books, and possibly filmstrips, records, and magazines that contain information about people around the world. Reading is the easiest way to travel to faraway places. Maps of other countries are interesting to study, and can tell you a lot about the land, rivers, and other physical characteristics of the world.

Many schools and clubs sponsor International Festivals. At one of these events you walk from table to table, each featuring a specific country, and sample the native foods while viewing displays of crafts and clothing from that country. These festivals are an enjoyable way to learn about other countries.

Museums usually have some international exhibits, and are a good source of information about foreign countries.

Make Friends with People from Other Countries

Write a "Pen Pal" in another country.

> International Pen Friends
> P.O. Box 65
> Brooklyn, New York 11229

U.S. Committee for UNICEF
331 East 38th Street
New York, N.Y. 10016

Encourage your family to host foreign students or visitors in your home during their stay in America, offering friendship and hospitality while learning about your guest's home country.

Join the international club at your school, if there is one. If not, help start one.

Help a refugee family settle into your community.

Refugee Resource Center
200 Park Avenue South
Room 1703
New York, N.Y. 10003

Befriend foreign students at your school. Their experience entering a strange school, without a good command of the English language, is very similar to the Peace Corps volunteer's experience entering his or her host country. Just as you hope your host country will welcome you when you arrive as a Peace Corps volunteer sometime in the future, so too should you welcome foreign students to your school and community.

Learn More About Your Own Culture

The second goal of the Peace Corps is to help promote a better understanding of Americans on the part of the peoples served. Peace Corps volunteers are often asked questions about the United States.

The more you know and understand about America, the better you can represent our country among the people of the world. Newspapers, magazines, trips to historical sites, and school courses in American and state history can help widen your view of America. Collecting stories and memories about the past from your friends and relatives is a fun way to learn about your country's history, as well as your personal history.

Develop a Skill or Interest

Peace Corps volunteers are assigned to specific jobs. Volunteers are matched with an assignment that utilizes their particular skills and knowledge. Expertise in such fields as sign language, beekeeping, knitting, the law, or mathematics can be used in the Peace Corps. So develop your interests, enjoy your hobbies, and join interesting clubs in preparation for future Peace Corps service.

Participate in Other Voluntary Activities

Peace Corps volunteers need to respect host country friends and co-workers as they work alongside them, without making fun of the cultural differences. They also need to know how to get along with other people. These skills can be developed through participation in service organizations such as 4-H, YMCA and YWCA, Girl and Boy Scouts, Campfire, Boys and Girls Clubs, and church groups. Some of these groups offer opportunities to learn about global issues and events. Local chapters of these organizations can be found in your telephone directory.

Opposite page: There are 4-H type programs in many countries, including the Philippines.

How You Can Help the Peace Corps 123

Help Other People

Hunger exists everywhere, even in America. Learn about the four basic food groups and make sure you eat a proper diet every day. For information, you can write:

> World Hunger Education Office
> 1317 G Street, N.W.
> Washington, D.C. 20005

Plant and harvest a garden. Donate food to a food bank or church food drive. Assist your community's "Meals on Wheels" program. Help at a soup kitchen. Become a Peace Corps Partner (see Chapter 9).

Many people around the world don't have a doctor or nurse nearby, and don't have good health care. Learn and practice good health habits. Be a Red Cross aide or candy striper at a hospital. You can check with your local hospital for details or write:

> American Red Cross
> 17th and D Streets, N.W.
> Washington, D.C. 20006

The Peace Corps, with twenty-five years of distinguished service, continues to fill a need in the world of the 1980s and beyond. People today realize that we must look beyond ourselves and help the needy, the poor, and the hungry wherever they may live.

The Peace Corps has helped make the world a better place for millions of people through the efforts of individual Americans, who believed that their efforts, however small, could make a difference. Perhaps Dr. Tom Dooley, a doctor who spent his life working with the poor and suffering in Asia, said it best:

> "I am only one, but I am one.
> I cannot do everything, but I can do something.
> What I can do, I ought to do,
> And what I ought to do, by the grace of God,
> I will do."

Index

AAU/USA Junior Olympics, 118
Agency for International Development (AID), 68
American Red Cross, 124
Application, volunteer (Peace Corps), 55

Birth of the Peace Corps, 10-23
Boahene, Eugene, 98
Bukavu, Zaire, Peace Corps training center, 64

Cabanas, Honduras, 111
Cameroon, 43, 69
Carter, Vincent, 94
Central African Republic, 97-98
Children's International Summer Villages, Inc., 117
Chile, 90
Costa Rica, 107, 115

Dodd, Christopher, 84, 87
Dooley, Tom, 125
Dowdowa, Ghana, 18

Ecuador, 35, 42-43, 44, 99, 104, 108-109, 118
Evergreen, Colorado, Peace Corps training program at, 58-60

Fiji, 85
Foreign Assistance Act, Percy Amendment to, 42
Foster Parents Plan/High School International Education Program, 116
4-H, 122, 123
Friendship Force International, 116

Ghana, 14, 18, 19, 28, 98, 100
Girl Scouts, 103, 106-107, 117
Goals, Peace Corps, 18, 86, 121
Goma, Zaire, 64
Guatemala, 38, 40, 41, 44

Haiti, 26
Headquarters, (Peace Corps), 56

Honduras, 51, 100, 109-111
Humphrey, Hubert H., 10, 14

ICE Almanac, 48-49
Information Collection and Exchange (ICE) program, 46-49
International Festivals, 120
International Pen Friends, 120
International Student Exchange, 114
International Voluntary Services, 10, 12, 13
Interview with Peace Corps recruiter, 55-56

Jamaica, 36
James, William, 10, 12

Kakamba, Zaire, 66-79
Kennedy, John F., 10, 14-16, 17, 19, 86, 88
Kenya, 49, 88, 102, 119
Khartoum, Sudan, 57, 62
Kilembu, Zaire, 70
Kinshasa, Zaire, 63
Korea, 94

Languages, taught by Peace Corps, 60, 64, 119
Livingston, Tom, 10, 17-18, 19

Malaysia, 31, 35, 90, 111
Mali, 49
May, Abe, 95
"Meals on Wheels" program, 124
Michigan, University of, 14
Mobility International, USA, 116
Montserrat, 25
Morocco, 44, 45

National Council of Returned Peace Corps Volunteers, 86
National Handicapped Sports and Recreation Association, 118
Nepal, 44, 103-107
Niger, 30
Nigeria, 36

Oak Park, Illinois, participation in Peace Corps Partnership Program, 109
Offices, area (Peace Corps), 56
Olympic Youth Camp, 117
"Operation Crossroads," 12-13

Paraguay, 95, 102
Partnership Program, Peace Corps, 103-112
Peace Corps Act, 10, 18, 42
Peace Corps Times, 48, 49
Percy, Charles, 42
Percy Amendment to Foreign Assistance Act, 42
Philippine Islands, 12, 36, 37, 46, 47, 48, 91-94, 102
"Point Four Youth Corps" plan, 14
President's International Youth Exchange, 116
Purposes of the Peace Corps, 18, 86, 121

Refugee Resource Center, 121
Reuss, Henry, 10, 14
Robinson, James H., 10, 12
Ruppe, Loret Miller, *vi-vii,* 36

San Jeronimo, Honduras, 109
Save the Children Federation, Inc., 119-120

Shriver, Sargent, 16, 17, 84
Sierra Leone, 13, 22, 27, 36-37, 38-39, 44, 53
Sioux City, Iowa, participation of Boys Club in Peace Corps Partnership Program, 111
Sport for Understanding, 117, 118
Student Exchange Programs, 114, 116
Sudan, 56-62

Telephone number, Peace Corps, 54
Thailand, 29
Thomas, USS, 12
Thomasites, 12
Togo, 20, 21, 41, 54, 86, 101
Tonga, 46, 48
Training program, Peace Corps, 58-60, 64, 66
Truk Islands, 95
Tsongas, Paul, 84, 89
Turkey, 90

U.S. Committee for UNICEF, 121
U.S. Information Agency, Youth Exchange Staff, 116

Villarrica, Paraguay, 95-97
Volunteer, Peace Corps, how to become a, 50-62
Volunteers, Peace Corps, returned, 83-90

Walkerton, Indiana, participation of students in Peace Corps Partnership Program, 104, 108-109

Western Samoa, 44, 57, 90
Westminster, Colorado, participation of Girl Scouts in Peace Corps Partnership Program, 103-107
Women, Peace Corps help for, 38-45
World Hunger Education Office, 124

YMCA, 122
Youth for Understanding/Peace Corps Scholarship Program, 114
YWCA, 122

Zaire, 63-82